CorelDRAW
On Command

Michael Ward
with Jeff Koch

NRP
NEW RIDERS
PUBLISHING

New Riders Publishing,
Carmel, Indiana

CorelDRAW! On Command

by Michael Ward with Jeff Koch

Published by:

New Riders Publishing
11711 N. College Ave., Suite 140
Carmel, IN 46032

Printed in the United States of America 1 2 3 4 5 6 7 8 9

Library of Congress Cataloging-in-Publication Data is available on request.

Publisher
David P. Ewing

Acquisitions Editor
Brad Koch

Managing Editor
Tim Huddleston

Series Director
Cheri Robinson

Production Editor
Lisa D. Wagner

Editors
Geneil Breeze
Nancy Sixsmith

Technical Editors
James Karney
Dennis Sanner

Production
Scott Boucher
Mark Enochs
Brook Farling
Phil Kitchel
Laurie Lee
Linda Seifert
Sandra Shay
Lisa Wilson
Allan Wimmer

Indexer
Loren Malloy

Trademark Acknowledgements

Warning and Disclaimer

Table of Contents

Introduction

CorelDRAW! On Command provides an instant resource for the information you need to use CorelDRAW productively. It presents information in a visual, intuitive, and easy-to-understand format. Kept close to your computer, *CorelDRAW! On Command* can provide the immediate information you need to create professional drawings. Each chapter's "Notes" section includes hints for optimizing your work.

Who Should Use *CorelDRAW! On Command*?

Many people who use CorelDRAW need help remembering the most efficient way to do a task. They also appreciate learning new shortcuts and tips for improved performance. If you are just learning CorelDRAW, this book presents the information you need to learn in an easy-to-follow format. *CorelDRAW! On Command* meets the needs of a wide range of users, including:

- Those who use CorelDRAW infrequently

- Those who use some aspects of CorelDRAW frequently, but other features rarely

- Beginners who need a simple and easy-to-use reference for performing specific tasks

- The curious who want to explore the CorelDRAW environment

- Experienced users

CorelDRAW beginners will find *CorelDRAW! On Command* to be an ideal companion to New Riders' *Inside CorelDRAW!, 3rd Edition*.

What is Included in *CorelDRAW! On Command*

Features designed into this unique reference include the following:

- Referenced step-by-step instructions for performing each essential task

- Tips and notes that you can use to improve your efficiency

- Cautions to help you avoid common problems

How Are the Tasks Organized?

CorelDRAW! On Command is organized into chapters that group related tasks together to help you find the information you need. To find which chapter is most likely to help you, think about your overall objective.

The first page of a chapter lists the tasks presented in this chapter. Each task begins by describing the reasons for performing the task in a segment called "Purpose." The next part of the task description, "Steps," shows you exactly how to perform the task. The elements you use for each step are discussed and the required actions are clearly explained. The final section of the task is entitled "Notes." This section provides tips and cautions to make your work easier.

The following descriptions are provided to help you locate the information you want:

Chapter 1, "Getting Started," introduces you to CorelDRAW basics and teaches you the fundamental skills you need to have to start using the program.

Chapter 2, "Drawing Lines and Curves," outlines the techniques you can use to create these basic drawing elements.

Chapter 3, "Drawing Rectangles and Ellipses," continues the discussion of basic drawing shapes. You learn how to combine different shapes and duplicate shapes to create interesting objects.

Chapter 4, "Creating Text," shows you how to use text to enhance your drawings. You learn to use all the text tools so that you can change a sheet of words into a logo.

Chapter 5, "Moving and Transforming Objects," teaches you how to change the objects you draw to create the effect you want.

Chapter 6, "Arranging and Aligning Objects," teaches you to use some of CorelDRAW's special features. You can create layers to show dimension or group objects together to form a new perspective.

Chapter 7, "Filling and Outlining Objects," teaches you to modify the outline and fill of an object to add texture, dimension and other creative effects to your drawing.

Chapter 8, "Using Special Effects," teaches you to add dimensional effects and also how to change perspective. You learn to use the Envelope option to stretch and distort objects.

Chapter 9, "Printing," shows you how to prepare your files to be printed within CorelDRAW or by a service bureau. You learn which options to use if you use a PostScript printer.

Chapter 10, "Managing Files," shows you how to organize, view, and save your files. You also learn to use AutoTrace and the CorelTRACE utility to prepare imported files for editing.

CHAPTER 1

Getting Started

Before you can use CorelDRAW successfully, you must have a basic understanding of some of the program's fundamental workings. This chapter introduces you to CorelDRAW. After you work through the tasks in this chapter, you will be ready to create professional looking drawings.

In this chapter, you learn about the following CorelDRAW basics:

- Understanding the CorelDRAW screen
- Using the CorelDRAW tools
- Opening a file
- Saving a file
- Setting up the page
- Hiding display settings
- Setting up the grid
- Setting preferences
- Selecting objects
- Using Preview

Understanding the CorelDRAW Screen

Purpose

Before you can successfully use CorelDRAW, you should have an understanding of the basic areas of its screen.

Steps

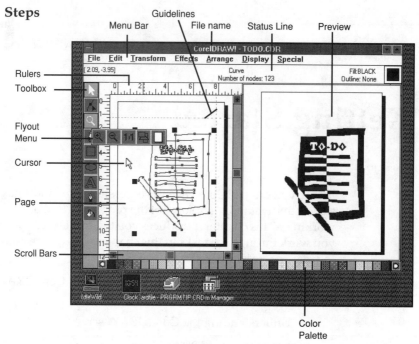

Rulers

Toolbox

Flyout
Menu

Cursor

Page

Scroll Bars

Color
Palette

Notes

The menu bar contains the pull-down menus from which you choose command options.

The status line contains information about the object that you are creating. Information such as coordinates, number, and dimension is given.

The scroll bars enable you to view different sections of the screen that are currently visible.

The ruler establishes the coordinates for your drawing. You can judge the placement of objects.

The toolbox contains the tools you use to draw and edit. The toolbox contains the following tools: Pick, Shape, Zoom, Pencil, Rectangle, Ellipse, Text, Outline, and Fill.

Opening a File

Purpose

This task enables you to open a new file or retrieve an existing file.

Steps

To open a new file, choose <u>N</u>ew from the <u>F</u>ile menu or press **Alt-F, N**.

To open an existing file, follow these steps:

1. From the <u>F</u>ile menu, select <u>O</u>pen or press **Ctrl-O**.

2. Click the name of the file you want to open. CorelDRAW shows you the directory you last used. To change directories, press the up arrow.

Saving a File

Purpose

This task teaches you the way to save a new file or save changes to an existing file.

Steps

1. From the <u>F</u>ile menu, select <u>S</u>ave. Select Save <u>A</u>s to create a new version of an existing file.

2. You are prompted to enter a file name in the Save Drawing dialog box.

3. Click OK to save the file.

Setting Up the Page

Purpose

You can control the size and the shape of the printable page. The page orientation can be horizontal (<u>L</u>andscape) or vertical (Po<u>r</u>trait). You can select from seven preset sizes and a custom size.

Steps

1. From the File menu, select Page Setup, or double-click on the page border. The Page Setup dialog box appears.

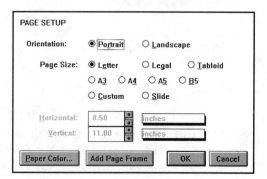

2. Select the Orientation for the printed page.

3. Select Page Size. You can select Letter, Legal, Tabloid, A3, A4, A5, B5, Custom, and Slide. The Slide option maintains the proper aspect ratio for 35mm slides.

4. If you selected Custom, set the page dimensions in the Horizontal and Vertical boxes. You can set the dimensions by using inches, picas, points, or millimeters.

5. Click OK.

Notes

 To make slides, set the Paper Color to black to simulate the effect of unexposed film.

You can approximate the effect of your design on colored paper by changing the preview paper color. Note that objects in CorelDRAW are opaque, whereas inks are transparent.

Hiding Display Settings

Purpose

You can turn off the ruler, status line, and color palette to give you a slightly larger active drawing area.

Steps

1. Select the **D**isplay menu.

2. Click on the settings you want to turn off. A check mark appears next to items that are turned on.

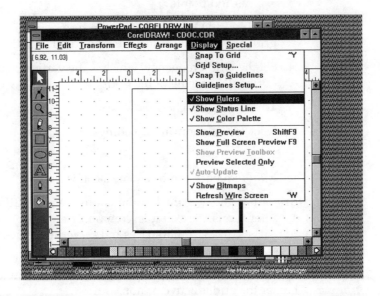

Notes

Turning off these elements is especially helpful if you must work on a small monitor.

Setting Up the Grid

Purpose

This feature enables you to create a grid so that you can align objects or draw multiple objects of the same size.

Steps

1. From the <u>D</u>isplay menu, select Gr<u>i</u>d Setup. The Grid Parameters dialog box appears.

2. Select the unit of measure that you want to use. You can select from the following units of measure:

   - inches
   - millimeters
   - points
   - picas and points

3. Set the Grid Origin, which is the zero point of the grid. The default setting is the bottom left of the page.

4. Set the Grid Frequency, which is the vertical and horizontal spacing of the grids.

5. To see the grid, click Show Grid.

6. Click OK to confirm the settings.

Notes

The Grid Frequency can be as fine as one point.

<u>H</u>orizontal and <u>V</u>ertical dimensions can be different. Computer forms, for example, commonly are designed on a grid that has 10 horizontal spaces and six vertical spaces to the inch.

The units for the Grid Setup appear on the Status Line, whether the grid is active or not.

 Double-clicking on the rulers displays the Grid Setup dialog box.

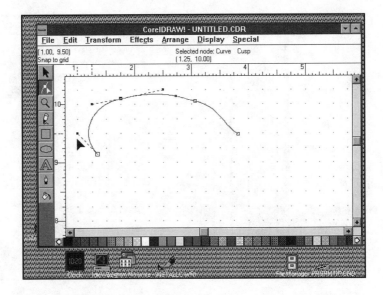

 Curve nodes and control nodes snap to grid points when moved if Snap to Grid is on.

Setting Guidelines

Purpose

You can add nonprinting guidelines to your work area so that you can align objects. Positioning is relative to grid origin, which by default is the lower left corner.

Steps

1. From the **D**isplay menu, select Guide**l**ines Setup. The Guidelines dialog box appears.

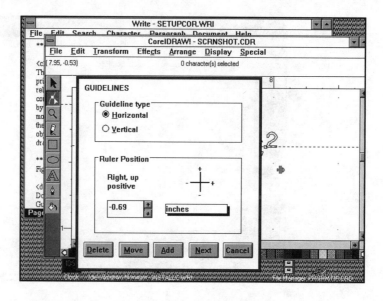

2. Select Guideline type and set the corresponding coordinate.

Notes

A simple way to create guidelines is to click on one of the rulers and drag the mouse cursor to the location at which you want the guideline to appear.

To delete a guideline, click on the guideline and drag it off the screen.

Text snaps to vertical guidelines based on its alignment setting. Centered text centers on the guideline; left and right text aligns to the edge of the guideline.

Use guidelines to align the handles of a curve. Guidelines also are useful for setting up a column grid for page layouts. You can align subscripts and superscripts with guidelines.

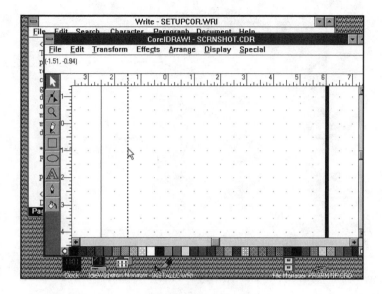

Setting Default Preferences

Purpose

The Preferences menu enables you to change a number of default settings within CorelDRAW.

Steps

1. From the **S**pecial menu, select Pr**e**ferences.

2. In the Preferences dialog box, enter the settings you prefer.

Notes

The Place Duplicate settings determine where a duplicate object is placed. When both are set to zero, the duplicate object is placed directly on top of the original object.

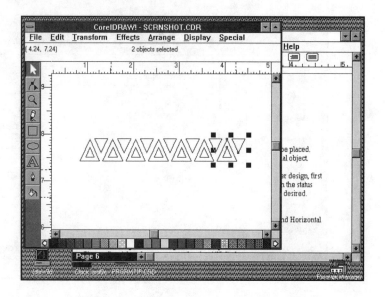

To produce a series of evenly spaced objects, such as for a border design, move the object the desired amount of space, noting this figure as displayed on the status line. Then set the displacement to the value, and duplicate the item as desired.

The Nudge setting determines how far an object is bumped by the arrow keys. Setting Nudge at the minimum value of .1 points is useful for precisely aligning objects. A larger value of .5 or 1 point is good for making fine adjustments without having to zoom in. Hold down the arrow key to move the object continuously.

The keyboard shortcut for setting Pre̲ferences is **Ctrl-J**.

Selecting a Single Object

Purpose

You must select an object to transform it or to change its fill and outline. You use the Pick tool to select objects or groups of objects.

Steps

1. Select the Pick tool.

2. Move the cursor to the object you want to select, and click once. (You must click on part of the outline of the object to select it.)

3. A set of eight black squares appears around the object. The black squares mark the boundary of the highlighting box for the object. Each of these squares is a handle that you can use to manipulate the object.

Notes

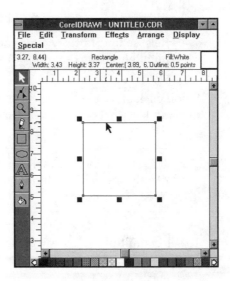

The highlighting box has two modes: stretch/scale mode, which is the default, and rotate/skew mode. In rotate/skew mode, eight arrows replace the eight squares. To switch between modes, click on the outline of the object. (For more information, see Chapter 5.)

When the Pick tool is active, use Tab to alternate through the objects. Tab moves from last to first based on the sequence of the object's creation. Pressing Shift-Tab selects the preceding object. Use this method if you must select an object directly underneath another object.

Selecting Multiple Objects

Purpose

You can select multiple objects by using the Shift-click or marquee selection methods.

Steps

To select multiple objects by using the Shift-click method, follow these steps:

1. Select the Pick tool.

2. Hold down the Shift key.

3. Click on the outline of the object(s) desired.

4. Release the Shift key after you are finished. The highlighting box expands to surround all the selected objects.

If you click on a selected object again while you hold down the Shift key, that object is deselected.

 The status line shows the number of items selected. If only one item is selected, the status line shows the type of object.

To select multiple objects by using the marquee select method, follow these steps:

1. Select the Pick tool.

2. Click the mouse button and drag the cursor. A dotted rectangle appears.

3. Release the mouse button after all the objects you want to select are within the rectangle. Objects are selected after you release the button.

Notes

An object must fit entirely inside the dotted rectangle—called a *marquee*—for it to be selected.

To deselect objects, hold down the Shift key as you drag the marquee.

Use the Edit menu's Select All option to select all objects.

To deselect all the objects, click in any open space. All highlighting boxes disappear.

You can move objects so far that they "fall" off the displayed screen. If you suspect that a file has such "lost" objects, use the Select All command to grab them so that they can be moved into view or deleted.

Using the Zoom Tools

Purpose

To have greater control over your drawings, you can magnify a portion of the drawing. After you are zoomed in, you can make changes in smaller increments. The Zoom tool contains a fly-out menu with five options.

Steps

To zoom in, follow these steps:

1. Select the + tool from the Zoom menu.

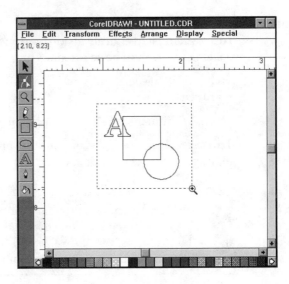

2. Drag a marquee box around the area you want to zoom.

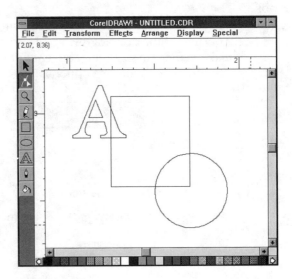

3. Release the mouse button. CorelDRAW executes the zoom after you release the mouse button. Maximum magnification is about 12 times actual size.

Notes

To zoom out, click on the - tool to zoom out to the previous magnification. If you have zoomed in to an area of a drawing several times to increase its magnification, the - tool takes you back one level at a time.

To see the object at actual size, click on the 1:1 tool to display the drawing at roughly the actual size view. The accuracy of this option depends on your monitor.

To show all objects, click on the Show All Objects tool to include all objects in one view. If the objects are too far apart to be shown in one view, a warning message displays.

To show the entire page, click on the Show Page tool. Some objects may be outside this view.

The right mouse button can be set for a 2x zoom. Use zoom out and zoom in to move from one side of a file to another. This method is faster and easier to control than the scroll bars.

Save As

The Save **A**s command enables you to save the existing file under another name. If that name is already in use, you receive a warning prompt. You need only type the file name; CorelDRAW adds the CDR extension.

Undoing and Repeating Commands

Purpose

With CorelDRAW, you can cancel or repeat the most recently used command.

Steps

To cancel a command, select **U**ndo from the **E**dit menu.

To repeat a command, select **R**epeat from the **E**dit menu.

Notes

To undo the Undo, select Redo from the Edit menu.

Only one level of Undo exists in CorelDRAW, so if you do something you did not want to do, use Undo immediately.

You cannot Undo zoom and pan or any file operations.

The keyboard shortcut for Undo is Alt-Backspace.

The keyboard shortcut for Redo is Alt-Enter.

The Edit menu's Repeat command repeats the most recent transformation or arrangement on the currently selected object(s). If you immediately select another object after you perform an action, Repeat performs the operation on the newly selected object.

Repeat can be used to group, combine, and arrange operations as well.

Use the Repeat command after rotating or skewing as the equivalent of a "nudge" command: rotate or skew some small increment, such as 1 degree. Then press Ctrl-R to repeat the operation as needed to achieve the desired transformation.

If you rotate an object, select another object, and then use Repeat, the second object is rotated around the first object's center of rotation, not its own.

The keyboard shortcut for Repeat is Ctrl-R.

Duplicating Objects

Purpose

You can create a duplicate of the selected object or objects.

Steps

From the Edit menu, select Duplicate.

A duplicate of the selected object or objects is created.

Notes

The position of the duplicate is determined by the Place Duplicate settings in the Preferences dialog box.

The keyboard shortcut for Duplicate is Ctrl-D.

Copying, Cutting, and Pasting

Purpose

You can use the Windows Clipboard to cut and paste objects. You can paste the objects into another CorelDRAW file, or into another Windows program that handles CorelDRAW clipboard files. See the *Technical Reference* for more details about cutting and pasting to specific programs.

Steps

1. Select the desired objects.

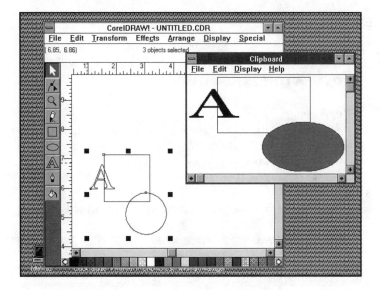

2. From the **E**dit menu select **C**opy or Cut to copy or cut the items to the Clipboard.

3. The **P**aste command pastes the items back into the same position in the file.

Notes

The clipboard has a limit of 64K when you copy or cut objects. If the objects exceed this limit, you see the warning CorelDRAW! Clipboard format too large to put on Clipboard. This warning means that the objects must be cut or copied in the Windows Metafile (WMF) format. If you receive the message Metafile too large to put on clipboard, however, then you exceeded even the Metafile limit, and the objects cannot be placed on the clipboard. You must then cut or copy fewer or simpler objects, or use the Export command to export the selected objects to a new CorelDRAW file.

A full clipboard slows things down, especially if limited memory is available. If you copy a simple object to the clipboard, this object overwrites the complex one and memory becomes available.

Shortcut keys for the Edit tools are as follows:

Copy   Ctrl-Ins

Cut   Shift-Del

Paste   Shift-Ins

Previewing Drawings

Purpose

You can preview the current drawing in a window beside the file. This preview shows how the drawing prints, within the limits of the screen display.

Steps

From the Display menu, select Show Preview.

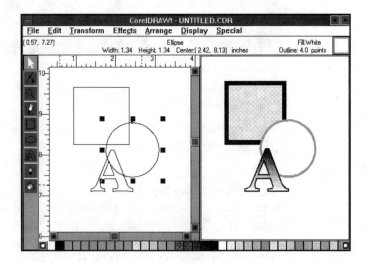

A preview of the drawing appears next to the open file.

Notes

If you click anywhere in the preview window, the object is redrawn. To stop the redrawing process, press any key or click anywhere outside the preview window. Use the **D**isplay menu's Preview Selected **O**nly option to reduce the time it takes to redraw or identify superimposed objects. This option previews only the currently selected objects.

The keyboard shortcut for previewing is Shift-F9.

If you select Auto-Update, the preview screen automatically redraws each time you modify the drawing. The default setting is on. You can change this option only while you are in preview mode.

Turn Auto-Update off when working with complicated files. Instead, click inside the Preview window when a redraw of the preview is desired.

To change the size and orientation of the preview window, drag the edge of the preview window. If the Preview window is a different size than the editing window, the preview is scaled accordingly.

To change the preview window to top-and-bottom view, drag the top or bottom of the preview window, and change the size of the window to less than half of the screen height. The preview window automatically changes to top-and-bottom orientation.

To see the previewed objects at maximum displayable size, select the Full Screen Preview option from the Display menu. With this setting enabled, the preview takes up the entire screen, even if the CorelDRAW window is less than the entire screen. Because this preview mode covers the menu bars, you won't be able to do any editing in this preview mode. Pressing any key returns you to editing mode.

The keyboard shortcut for Full Screen Preview is F9.

CHAPTER **2**

Drawing Lines and Curves

Both lines and curves are defined by nodes. A *node* is a point that acts as a handle to enable you to alter a line or object. Nodes appear as open boxes when an object is selected. They do not print. This chapter teaches you to create lines and curves in both Freehand and Bézier modes. The differences between the two modes are further explained as the chapter progresses. You also learn how to edit nodes and move control points.

In this chapter, you learn about the following operations:

- Drawing in Freehand and Bézier modes
- Drawing and shaping curves
- Defining and editing nodes and their control points

Drawing Lines in Freehand Mode

Purpose

This task teaches you to create single and multisegment lines in Freehand mode with the Pencil tool.

Steps
1. Select the Pencil tool (F5).

   Check the status bar to be sure that you are drawing in Freehand mode. (For information on changing modes, see Chapter 1.)

2. Move the cursor to the starting position.

3. Click the mouse button once to start the line. The cursor becomes a plus sign.

4. Move the cursor to where you want the line to end.

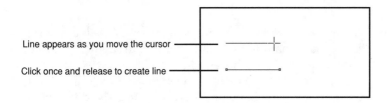

Line appears as you move the cursor ——

Click once and release to create line ——

5. Click the mouse button once to end the line. A line segment is created with a node on each end.

Notes

In either Bézier or Freehand mode, press and hold down the Control key to constrain the angle of the line to a multiple of the angle in the Constrain **A**ngle setting in the Preferences menu. This control is useful when you want to draw straight horizontal and vertical lines. Remember that you must release the mouse button while holding down the Control key for Constrain to be in effect.

Watch the status line as you draw a line. It gives you information such as line length, angle, and the exact position of the cursor. This status line only appears if you are in Freehand mode. It does not appear in Bézier mode.

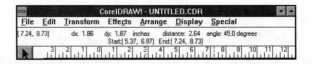

To create a multisegment line, double-click on the end of the first line and a new line begins.

Drawing Lines in Bézier Mode

Purpose

This task teaches you to create single and multisegment lines in Bézier mode with the Pencil tool.

Steps

1. Select the Pencil tool. Check the status bar to make sure that you are drawing in Bézier mode.

2. Move the cursor to the starting position.

3. Click the mouse button once to start the line.

4. Move the cursor to where you want the line to end.

5. Click the mouse button once to end the line. A line segment is created.

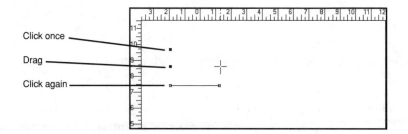

Click once
Drag
Click again

 If the mouse moves as you click to create a node, all line segments connected to that node are created as curves, not lines.

Notes

To create multisegment lines in Bézier mode, simply move the cursor to another location and click. A new line segment is created. You do not need to double-click the mouse.

To start a new, unconnected line segment in Bézier mode, press the space bar twice. This action changes the cursor to Pick and back to the drawing mode again.

To close an object, bring your final line segment back to the beginning node and click once. This operation works in both Freehand and Bézier modes. Only closed objects can be filled with a color or pattern. (AutoJoin under the Preferences menu determines how close you need to be to the beginning node for a curve to close.

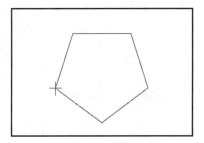

Drawing Curves in Freehand Mode

Purpose

This task teaches you how to create curved lines in Freehand mode. Drawing curves in Freehand mode is just like drawing curves on paper.

Steps

1. Select the Pencil tool. Check the status bar to be sure you are drawing in Freehand mode. (For information on changing modes, see Chapter 1.)

2. Move the cursor to the starting point of the curve.

3. Press and hold the mouse button down while moving the mouse.

4. CorelDRAW draws a path with the appropriate nodes to fit the mouse path. How closely CorelDRAW tracks

your drawing path and where it places the nodes is
controlled from the Preferences menu.

Drawing Curves in Bézier Mode

Purpose

This task teaches you how to create curved lines in Bézier
mode.

Steps

1. Select the Pencil tool. Check the status bar to make
   sure that you are drawing in Bézier mode.

2. Move the cursor to the starting point of the curve.

3. Press and hold down the mouse button to generate a
   starting node.

4. As you continue to hold down the mouse button,
   move the mouse. This action stretches the control
   points. (Node types and control points are discussed
   later in this chapter.)

5. Release the mouse button.

6. Move the cursor to the ending point of the curve.

7. Press the button and move the mouse to create and
   shape the curve.

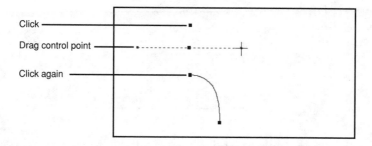

Notes

Although this method may not seem intuitive, it does produce
smooth, graceful curves with economical use of nodes.

Understanding Nodes and Control Points

Purpose

You can use several different types of curve nodes. Every curved line has at least two nodes. Each node on a curve is made up of at least one control point. You can change the shape of a curve by dragging its control points. You can move only one control point at a time; however, the other control point might move as well, depending on the type of node to which it is connected.

Three types of curve nodes that can be defined by the movement of their control points are as follows:

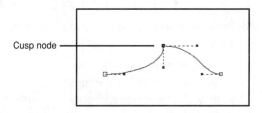

- **Cusp Nodes:** Control points of cusp nodes move freely and independently of each other. This freedom enables line segments to change direction sharply on either side of the node. Cusp nodes may have one or two control points.

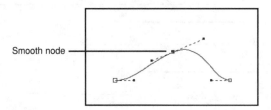

- **Smooth Nodes:** For smooth nodes, the control points can be of different distances from the node, but they always lie on a straight line that passes through the node.

If a smooth node is joined to a line segment, its control points are restricted to the direction of the line segment. Smooth nodes always have two control points.

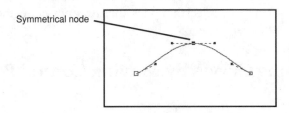

- **Symmetrical Nodes:** The control points for symmetrical nodes are the most restricted. The control points are connected by a single line, like smooth nodes, but are always an equal distance from the node. Thus both nodes always move together. Symmetrical nodes also always have two control points.

Reshaping Curves by Moving Nodes

Purpose

This task teaches you how to reshape curves by moving nodes with the Shape tool.

Steps

1. Select the Shape tool.

2. Click on the curve or line you want to reshape. The curve's nodes appear as open boxes.

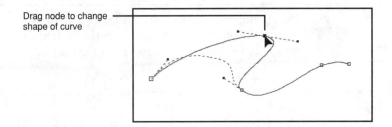

3. Click and drag a node to the desired location to change the shape of the curve.

Notes

To move more than one node at the same time, Shift-click or marquee-select the nodes, then drag any one of the highlighted nodes.

Reshaping Curves by Moving Control Points

Purpose

This task teaches you how to reshape curves by moving control points with the Shape tool.

Steps

1. Select the Shape tool.

2. Click on the curve you want to reshape. The curve's nodes appear.

3. Click on the node whose control points you want to move. The control points become visible.

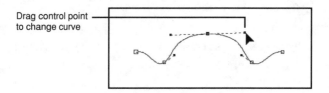

Drag control point to change curve

4. Click and drag the control points to change the curve's shape.

 When a control point sits directly on top of a node, it is very difficult to select. Hold down the Shift key to select only the control point and not the node.

Editing Nodes

Purpose

The Node Edit menu enables you to perform several editing operations on the selected nodes. You can add, delete, break, or align nodes; close, open or join paths; or change node or segment types.

Steps

1. With the Shape tool, select a node by clicking on it with the mouse or by using a marquee selection. To select more than one node, use a marquee or shift-click with the mouse.

   To deselect a node, click with the mouse or draw a marquee around already selected nodes. Shift-click to deselect a single node from a group.

2. Activate the Node Edit menu by double-clicking on a selected node. All menu options might not be available. Those that are available are shown in bold.

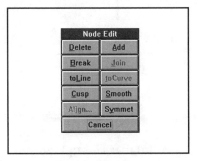

3. Choose the operation you want to perform. The options are discussed in the following section.

Notes

The options available for editing nodes are as follows:

- **Delete:** Removes all currently selected nodes. A node deleted at the end of a curve also deletes the last segment of that curve.

Deleting a node in the middle of a curve reshapes the curve.

- **Break:** Separates a curve into two segments at the selected node(s). If you double-click on a curve segment rather than a node, **B**reak separates the segment at the point touched by the mouse.

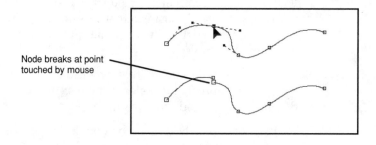

Node breaks at point touched by mouse

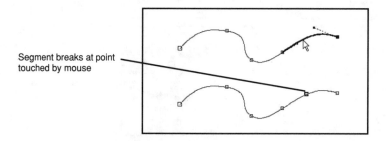

Segment breaks at point touched by mouse

- **toLine:** This option converts a curved segment into a straight line.

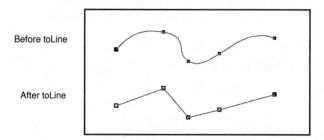

Before toLine

After toLine

- **Add:** Adds a node. Double-click on a node to highlight its associated segment, then choose **A**dd to place a node at the midpoint of the segment. Alternately, double-click on a segment and choose **A**dd to place a node at the point touched by the mouse.

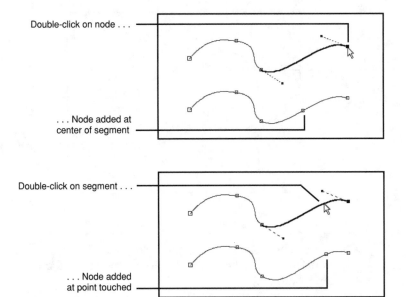

Double-click on node . . .

. . . Node added at center of segment

Double-click on segment . . .

. . . Node added at point touched

The segment associated with a node is the one between the highlighted node and the beginning node. The beginning node is slightly larger than the other nodes.

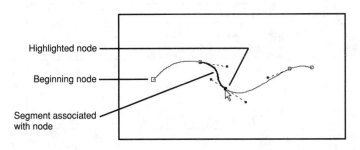

Highlighted node

Beginning node

Segment associated with node

- **Join:** Joins two, and only two, unconnected nodes. Any two nodes that are part of the same object and not currently connected to more than one line segment can be joined. If the two nodes to be joined are separated, the joined node is placed halfway between them.

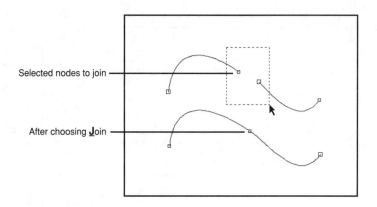

 To join nodes from two separate objects, the objects must first be combined. (See Chapter 6 for information on **C**ombine.)

If the end nodes of two paths are in exactly the same position, they might cancel each other out on the display, making them invisible. Check the status line to see how many unconnected paths a curve contains. To select two invisible nodes to join, drag a marquee box around the suspected location. The status line tells you if you have selected the hidden node.

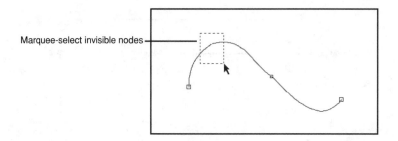

- **toCurve:** Converts a line node to a curve node. The shape of the curve does not change, but control points are created. You can then shape the curve as you want.

- **Cusp:** Converts a smooth or symmetrical node into a cusp node.

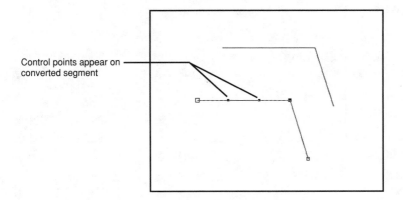

Control points appear on converted segment

- **Smooth:** Converts a symmetrical or cusp node into a smooth node.

- **Symmet:** Converts a smooth or cusp node into a symmetrical node.

- **Align:** Aligns two nodes on separate subpaths. The nodes can be aligned horizontally or vertically. Their control points can also be aligned, enabling the edges of two subpaths to meet. For example, you can use Align to match up the borders of two states when drawing a map.

 If you have gaps when aligning paths, "stitch up" the gap by adding nodes to either side of the gap and then aligning the new nodes.

If you want to align the edges of two separate objects, combine them into a single object, align nodes, and then break the objects apart.

You can edit only the nodes of one object at a time. Nodes of grouped objects cannot be edited.

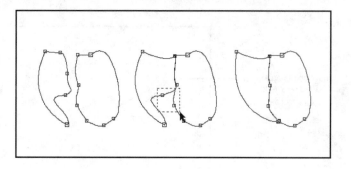

CHAPTER 3

Drawing Rectangles and Ellipses

Almost every object is composed of a few basic shapes, such as rectangles and ellipses. In CorelDRAW, rectangles and ellipses are primary objects, or predefined shapes. They remain primary objects unless you convert them to curves. Because they are primaries, they behave differently than free-form objects. This chapter teaches you to create and modify rectangles and ellipses.

In this chapter, you learn the following operations:

- Creating rectangles, squares and triangles
- Rounding corners
- Creating ellipses and circles
- Drawing arcs and wedges

Creating Rectangles

Purpose

This task teaches you how to create rectangles.

Steps

1. Select the Rectangle tool.

2. Place the cursor where you want the rectangle to begin.

3. Press the mouse button and drag the mouse to create the rectangle shape you want.

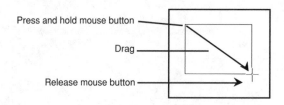

Press and hold mouse button

Drag

Release mouse button

4. Release the mouse button.

Notes

To draw a square, press and hold down the Control key as you drag the cursor. Be sure to release the mouse button *before* you release the Control key.

Hold down the Shift key as you drag the mouse to draw a rectangle that is centered around the original mouse position. Press Ctrl-Shift to draw a centered square.

Rounding Corners

Purpose

After you create a rectangle, you can round the corners by using the Shape tool.

Steps

1. Select the Shape tool.

2. Click on the rectangle you want to modify with the Shape tool.

3. Click and drag one of the corner nodes of the rectangle toward the center of the rectangle.

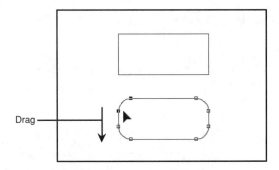

Drag

4. Release the mouse button.

   To remove the rounded corners, drag one of the nodes away from the center of the rectangle.

To make it easier to draw a series of rounded rectangles with the same corner radius, turn **S**nap to Grid on. The nodes automatically snap to the grid increments as you move them. (See Chapter 1 for more information on **S**nap to Grid.)

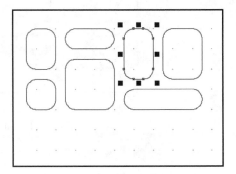

Be sure that you draw the rectangle to the desired shape with the Rectangle tool. If you stretch the rectangle before or after its corners are rounded, the corners are distorted. You can enlarge or reduce the rectangle without distorting the corners.

Drawing Triangles

Purpose

You can create triangles by using Node Edit, which you learned in Chapter 2.

Steps

1. Draw a rectangle and select it.

2. Convert the rectangle to a curve with the Convert to Curves command. (For more information on this command, see Chapter 6.)

3. Select the Shape tool.

4. Add a node midway along one of the line segments.

❶ Create rectangle

❷ Convert to curves and add node

❸ Delete corner node

❹ Resulting triangle

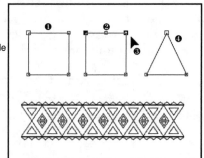

5. Delete the two corner nodes of that segment to create the triangle.

Creating Ellipses and Circles

Purpose

This task teaches you how to create ellipses.

Steps

1. Select the Ellipse tool.

2. Place the cursor where you want the ellipse to begin.

3. Press and hold down the mouse button.

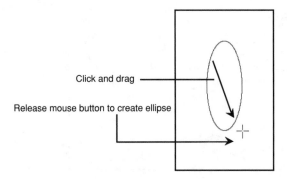

Click and drag

Release mouse button to create ellipse

4. Drag the cursor to create the desired shape.

5. Release the mouse button.

Notes

To draw a circle, press and hold down the Control key as you drag the cursor. Be sure to release the mouse button *before* you release the Control key.

Hold down the Shift key as you drag the mouse to draw an ellipse that is centered around the original mouse position. Press Ctrl-Shift to draw a centered circle.

Drawing Arcs and Wedges

Purpose

After you create an ellipse, you can modify the ellipse to form a pie or wedge shape with the Shape tool.

Steps

1. Select the Shape tool.

2. Click on the ellipse you want to modify. A single node appears.

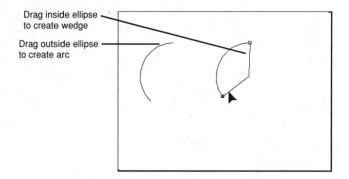

Drag inside ellipse to create wedge

Drag outside ellipse to create arc

3. Click and drag the node to modify the ellipse. Drag the node outside the ellipse to create an arc. Drag the node inside the ellipse to create a pie wedge. You can alternate freely between the two.

 Press and hold down the Control key as you drag the mouse to constrain the wedge or arc to 15-degree increments.

Notes

Because wedges and arcs are distorted ellipses, CorelDRAW remembers the undistorted ellipse shape. Thus the highlight box for a wedge or arc includes the full ellipse shape. This feature makes it easy to align the wedges of a pie graph, for example.

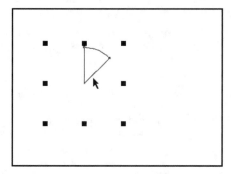

To select a wedge or arc by using the marquee select technique, you must completely surround the area that was occupied by the undistorted ellipse to select the object.

CHAPTER 4

Setting and Manipulating Type

In this chapter, you learn to handle CorelDRAW's many tools for setting type and manipulating it. You can use CorelDRAW to type a few words with no more thought than if you were using the simplest of word processors. Or you can use its many tools to craft a page worthy of a journeyman typesetter.

This chapter takes you through the subtle controls that can turn a word into a logo and change a page from a sheet of words into design. The many type tools in CorelDRAW help you communicate more effectively. They are easy to use after you know a few key words and ideas.

In the screen examples, the typeface names have been re-named from their default CorelDRAW names to their more common typeface names.

Use the the Text tool to create text. The three types of text are Text string, Paragraph text, and Symbols.

Using the Text String

Purpose

Use Text string for a few words, headlines, captions, callouts, and text you want to manipulate with the Effect tools.

Steps

1. Click on the Text tool, and the cursor changes to a cross.

2. Position the cursor on the screen where you want the text to appear.

3. Click to access the text dialog box.

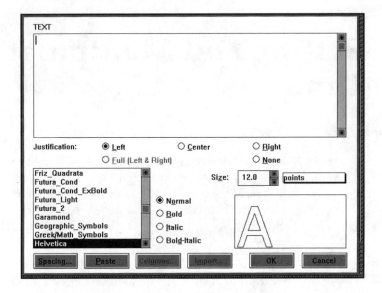

4. Enter the text string in the text window at the top of the dialog box. You can enter text in two ways: you can type from the keyboard, or you can paste from another application. You can enter up to 250 characters in the text string mode.

Entering the Text String with the Keyboard

Purpose

You can type in text directly from the keyboard to use as a text string for design and manipulation.

Steps

1. Place the cursor in the Text box. To do this, either click in the box or press Tab until the cursor appears in the Text Entry window.

2. Type in the text you want to place.

3. Press Enter to start a new line.

Pasting Text to the Text String

Purpose

You also can paste text to the Text Entry window from the Windows Clipboard, by using the Paste button at the bottom of the screen.

Steps

1. From another Windows program, such as Write, highlight the desired text.

2. Use Cut or **C**opy to place it on the clipboard.

3. Access the text dialog box, and click on the **P**aste button; or press Shift–Insert.

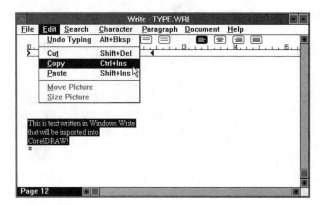

Notes

The limit for string text is 250 characters. Any text over this limit is not accepted. Line returns, spaces, and punctuation count as characters.

The keyboard shortcut to activate the Text tool is F8.

Selecting a Typeface

Purpose

Use the Typeface list box found in the Text dialog box to select a typeface. A preview of the first two letters of the text will appear in the preview window.

Steps

1. Activate the Typeface selection box.

2. To select the typeface, use the scroll bars to move through the list, and then click on the desired typeface; or type the first letter of the desired typeface. The listing then jumps to the first typeface that begins with that letter.

3. Select the text attributes you want for the text string:

   • **Type Size**. Described in points (72 points to one inch). Type is not, however, measured by the size of its capital letters. It is measured by the space it occupies from the top of its tallest ascender to the bottom of its longest descender.

   To select the type size in points, type a number in the Size box, or click on the up and down arrows. Type size must be between .07 and 1440 points (about 20 inches high).

 Text can be scaled even larger than 1440 points, but the results are sometimes unpredictable.

   • **Type Style**. Select Bold, Normal, Italic and Bold-Italic faces for the selected font, if they are available.

   • **Justification**. Can be set to Left, Right, Centered, or None (no alignment). Justification begins from the position of the cross hair when you clicked to get the key, therefore, if you change the justification mode the string shifts position horizontally.

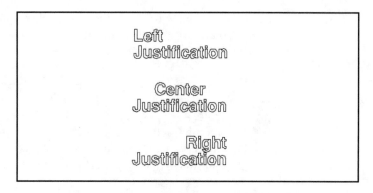

- **Spacing**. Click on the Spacing button to call up the Text Spacing dialog box. With this box, you can control the following three types of text spacing:

  - Inter-Character, which controls the spacing between individual characters. The default setting is 0.

  - Inter-Word, which controls the spacing between words. The default setting is 1 em.

  - Inter-Line, which controls the spacing between lines, or leading. This is calculated as a percentage of the face height. The default setting is 100%.

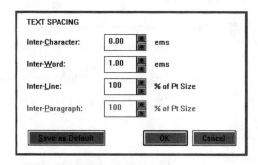

You can save custom settings by clicking on the <u>S</u>ave as Default button. The settings remain in effect for that file until you change them.

For most typefaces, the default interword spacing is too wide. A setting of .60 to .70 looks better. Usually the intercharacter setting can be tightened as well. An intercharacter setting of −.05 is good. Set this even tighter when you create headline-size text.

> Text at normal word and
> letter spacing settings
>
> Text at preferred word and
> letter spacing settings

Notes

Some typefaces do not have lowercase letters. If you type lowercase letters in these faces, they are displayed as periods.

Modifying Text

Purpose

You can modify the spacing, leading, and kerning of text after it is created by using the Node Edit tool. Moving individual letters farther apart is *spacing* them; moving them closer together is *kerning*.

Steps

1. Activate the Node Edit tool (F10).

2. Select the string. (Nodes appear at the bottom left corner of each letter.)

3. Select the characters you want to move. Shift-click or marquee select multiple characters.

4. Click and drag these nodes to move the letters.

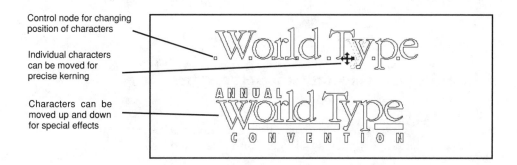

Control node for changing position of characters

Individual characters can be moved for precise kerning

Characters can be moved up and down for special effects

Notes

Hold down the Control key to constrain the characters to their baseline. They only move horizontally. If you move a character off the baseline, press Control while you move and the character jumps back to the baseline.

You also can nudge characters with the cursor keys. (See Chapter 2 for details on the Nudge function.)

 When justification is left, right, or centered, the first character of a string remains in a fixed horizontal position. To move this character relative to the others, set justification to None.

Editing String Text

Purpose

CorelDRAW makes it easy for you to edit string text you may already have modified or manipulated.

Steps

1. Highlight the text string with the Pick tool.

2. Select the Edit Text command from the Edit menu.

3. In the text dialog box that appears you can change copy, type face, type size, or another aspect of the text string.

Notes

The keyboard shortcut to edit text is Ctrl-T.

Changing Individual Character Attributes

Purpose

You may want to give individual letters or characters special attributes, such as a larger point size or a baseline shift.

Steps

To select the Character Attributes dialog box, double-click on a highlighted character's node. In this box you can change the typeface, type style, and type size of individual letters. You also can change the position of a letter in the **H**orizontal and **V**ertical Shift boxes. The Character **A**ngle box enables you to rotate a character a specific degree amount.

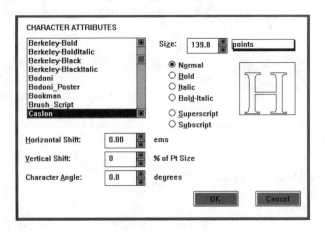

When one or more characters are highlighted, you also can access this box by clicking on C**h**aracter Attributes in the **E**dit menu.

Notes

Any change made in the Character Attributes dialog box applies to all highlighted characters, but only those values that you change are affected. For example, if you rotate two characters that have different point sizes, they are both rotated by the same amount, but their point sizes do not change.

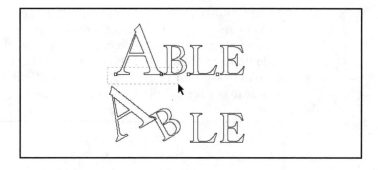

String text can be rotated, skewed, and stretched like any other object (see Chapter 5). The Envelope, Perspective and Extrude commands also can be applied to text (see Chapter 8). As long as you do not convert text to curves, you can still edit it.

 If you change the point size of all the characters in the string through the Character Attributes dialog box, the point size indicated on the status line reflects the original size of the letters, not the changed size.

Text Handles

When Node Edit mode is activated, two text handles appear at the bottom of the string. These are used to interactively change the spacing between characters, words, and lines.

(Lengthening a line using the normal highlighting box handles distorts the type.) For intercharacter spacing, drag the horizontal handle to increase or decrease character spacing. Hold down the control key and drag the horizontal handle to increase or decrease interword spacing. And Drag the vertical handle to change interline spacing, or leading.

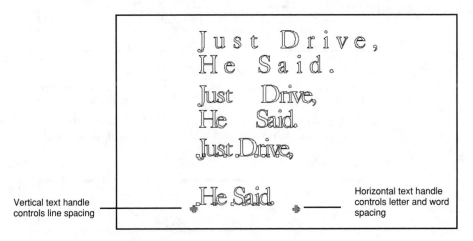

Vertical text handle controls line spacing

Horizontal text handle controls letter and word spacing

Using Paragraph Text

Purpose

Paragraph text mode is used for larger amounts of text—up to 4000 characters. Text can be entered in the text window, pasted from the clipboard, or imported from any ASCII text file.

Steps

1. Select the Text tool.

2. Click and drag the cursor. This creates a bounding box that holds your text.

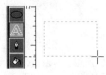

3. Enter the text by typing, pasting, or importing (see the following tasks).

Notes

The text you input fills the box and wraps to the next line automatically. Any text that cannot fit in the box is not shown, but remains part of the paragraph text (up to the 4000 character limit).

Text displayed in the paragraph block uses a generic typeface. The actual typeface appears in the preview screen.

All the settings for string text also can be applied to paragraph text. In addition, you can control the spacing between paragraphs within the text file. Paragraph text can be justified so that the right and left margins are even. You cannot change the attributes of individual letters of paragraph text.

A paragraph block can be rotated or skewed, just like any other object. If you skew the paragraph, only the box is slanted, not the text. The text is stepped, but is not distorted.

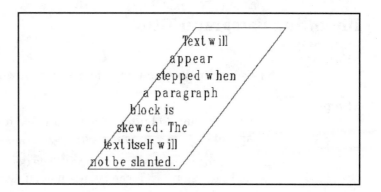

 CorelDRAW does not hyphenate automatically. To avoid gaps in justified type you must manually hyphenate your text.

This paragraph text has been manually hyphenated to avoid excessive gaps when the text is left and right justified.

This paragraph text has been man-ually hyphenated to avoid exces-sive gaps when the text is left and right justified.

Use paragraph text for larger blocks of type that you do not want to be distorted, such as the body type of an ad.

Importing Paragraph Text

Purpose

You also can import paragraph text from any ASCII file.

Steps

1. Click the Import button. The Import Text menu appears.

2. Select the file you want to import. The default path and extension, .TXT, can be modified, if needed.

3. Click on Import. Stretch the block to accommodate the text.

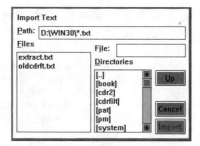

 Do not forget the 4000-character limit for paragraph text. If the text you import has more than 4000 characters, it is truncated.

Creating Multiple Columns

Purpose

Paragraph text can be set in up to 8 columns. The Gutter Width setting determines the amount of space between the columns.

Steps

1. From the Paragraph text dialog box, click on Columns. A dialog box appears.

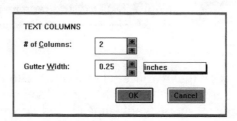

2. Select the number of columns and the Gutter **W**idth.

3. Click OK.

```
Paragraph  text    between      the
can be set in up   columns. In this
to eight columns.  example there is
The gutter setting 1/4"    between
determines  the    columns.
amount of space
```

Editing Paragraph Text

Purpose

CorelDRAW makes it easy for you to edit paragraph text you may already have modified or manipulated.

Steps

1. Click on the outline of the paragraph block to select it.

2. Select Edit **T**ext from the **E**dit menu.

3. Because the text size does not change if you drag the paragraph block, you must use the Edit **T**ext command to change the size of paragraph text.

 You cannot apply the Envelope, Perspective, and **E**xtrude effects to paragraph text.

Notes

Use the marquee-select technique to nudge a line of Paragraph text. With Left, Right or Left, and Right justification, you can nudge the line up and down. If the justification is set to None, you can nudge left and right as well.

Using Symbol Text

Purpose

CorelDRAW is packaged with many useful symbols that you may want to use in your drawings.

Use symbols as a starting point for more complex art. The wrench shown below was selected from the Tools symbol font, then extruded and colored.

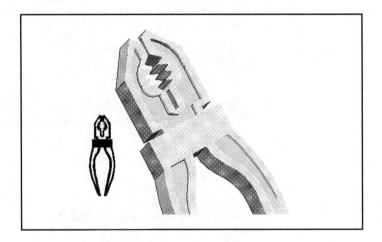

Steps

1. Select the Text tool.

2. When the cross cursor appears, hold down the Shift key and click. The Symbols dialog box appears. On the right is a list of the available symbol fonts.

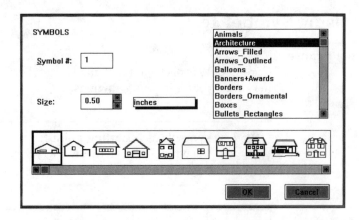

3. Select the symbol fonts you want to use. At the bottom of the symbols screen is a visual display of the symbols in the selected font.

4. Select the symbol you want to use. You can scroll through the symbols by using the arrow buttons and slider.

5. Set the symbol size. The size can be set from .1 to 20 inches.

6. Click OK. The symbol you choose is created in the drawing area as an object, which you size and modify like any other object.

Use the Symbol function for text-based symbol fonts (Zapf Dingbats/Dixieland, Carta/Geographic Symbols, Sonata/Musical) when those symbols are not part of a text block. The symbols display more accurately as objects than as text, especially in large sizes.

Some symbol fonts can be converted by WFNBOSS into text fonts; see the discussion that follows later in this chapter.

If you use a large number of identical symbols in a drawing, such as a map or chart, create a palette on-screen of the symbols you are using. Then use Ctrl-D to quickly copy these symbols without having to go back repeatedly to the Symbol menu.

Fitting Text to Path

This command enables you to fit text to the outline of any non-text object.

Steps

1. Use the Pick tool and Shift key to select the text object and the second object.

2. Select Fit Text to Path from the Arrange menu. The text aligns itself along the outline of the object.

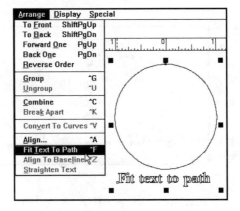

Notes

If you draw the object by dragging down and left, or up and right, the text is placed inside the object. If the object is drawn down and right, or up and left, the text is placed outside the object. You do not need to remember how you drew the object, however. To switch between inside and outside, use the Mirror function to reverse the path object.

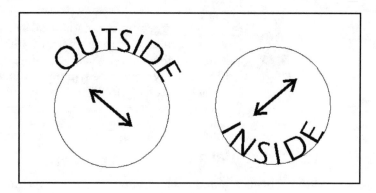

The justification of the text determines how it is placed on a path. Left justification or None causes the text to be aligned with the starting node of the path. Center justification aligns the text with the center of the path, and Right aligns the text with the end of the path. If the text is longer than the path, it makes another "lap" around the path.

Starting node of path

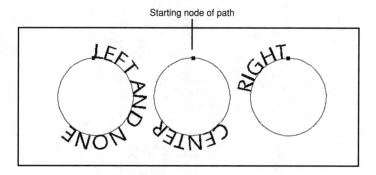

You must allow extra space between letters on a concave path, and tighten kerning on a convex path. You do not need to straighten the text before kerning, just drag the handle and use the Fit **T**ext To Path command again.

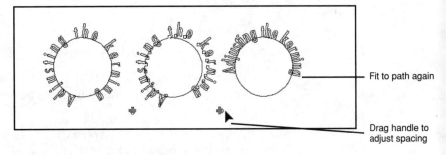

Fit to path again

Drag handle to adjust spacing

To fit text to another letter, use the Con<u>v</u>ert to Curves command in the <u>A</u>rrange menu to first convert that letter to an object.

You can adjust the spacing and angle of individual letters that have been fit to a path. To change the angle, double-click on the letter in the Pick mode to call up the Character Attributes dialog box.

The keyboard shortcut for Fit <u>T</u>ext to Path is Ctrl-F.

Use either the <u>E</u>dit menu's <u>U</u>ndo command or <u>S</u>traighten Text from the <u>A</u>rrange menu to take text off the path. <u>S</u>traighten Text, however, loses any kerning done previously. In addition, if you rotated the object and the text together, the straightened text is set at an angle, in a new position.

Lettering Two Lines of Type on a Circle

Purpose

Fit <u>T</u>ext to Path often is used to place text at the top and bottom of a circle or ellipse. To do this, you must make two circles. The distance between the inner and outer circles must equal the height of the text you are fitting.

Steps

1. Create the first circle.

2. Make a duplicate of the first circle.

3. Resize the second circle. Hold down the shift key to keep the two circles centered while you are doing this.

   Remember, the space between the circles must be equal to the height of the text.

4. Fit the top text to the inner circle.

   If the text appears on the wrong side of the circle, use the mirror command to reverse the circle, and fit again.

5. Fit the bottom type to the outer circle.

Notes

To adjust the position of the lettering, select one of the strings and the outer circle, and rotate the two objects. A temporary rectangle is handy to position the type. Once everything is perfect, set the fill and stroke of the two circles to none (unless you want them to print). Do this instead of deleting them, so that you can make text changes later if needed.

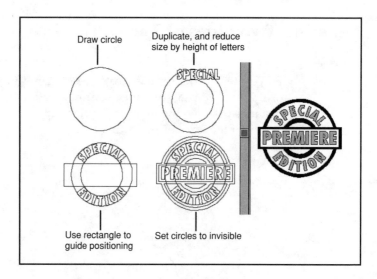

To fit text completely around a circle, you must do a little math. Create the circle, then note its diameter from the status line. Multiply the diameter by Pi to get the circumference. (Use the Windows Scientific calculator.) The result is the length the text must be to completely wrap around the circle. Size or letterspace your text to this length and allow for some space between the first and last characters. You can do this by first drawing a rectangle to the required length, and then sizing the text to match.

Copying Text Attributes

Purpose

You can copy the attributes of one text string to another by using the Copy Style From command in the Edit menu.

Steps

1. Select the text you want to copy the attributes to.

2. Select Copy Style From in the Edit menu. Copy Style From appears.

3. Check Text Attributes in the Copy Style menu, and click on OK. A FROM arrow then appears on the screen.

4. Move the tip of this arrow to the outline of the text you want to copy from, and click. The size, face, style, leading, and spacing are copied.

Any modifications of individual characters are not copied, nor are any stretch or skew operations. The **R**epeat command repeats this operation, making it easy to modify multiple type strings.

Extracting and Merging Back Text

Purpose

This feature enables you to work on text strings and paragraph text outside of a CorelDRAW file. CorelDRAW can "extract" text objects from one file and place them in an editable ASCII text file, which later can be "merged" back into the original CorelDRAW file.

Steps

To extract the text:

1. Select E**x**tract from the **S**pecial menu. The E**x**tract dialog box appears.

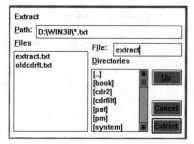

2. Give the file a name. This file is separate from the CorelDRAW file, so give it any name you want.

3. Click on E**x**tract.

 Do not save any changes to the CorelDRAW file between the time you E**x**tract and **M**erge-Back. If you do, you cannot merge back.

4. In a word processor, such as Windows Write or Notepad, edit the file. A numeral appears before each string or paragraph, and an "end-of-string" code— <CDR>—follows after. Do not touch these numerals or codes.

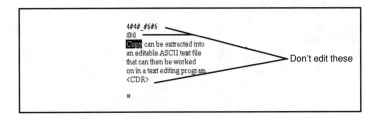

5. When you are finished editing the text, save it in ASCII format (simply saving it in Notepad is all right).

To merge the text back into the CorelDRAW file:

6. In the CorelDRAW file, select **M**erge-Back from the **S**pecial menu. The **M**erge-Back dialog box appears.

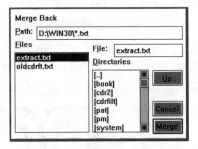

7. Pick your text file from the list and click on Merge. The revised text is merged into the CorelDRAW file. If you changed the length of any of the text strings, you must rearrange the elements in your file.

If you are making a foreign language version of an existing CorelDRAW file, **M**erge-Back and E**x**tract are useful. But other less specialized uses for this feature exist as well. CorelDRAW slows down considerably when it handles large paragraph blocks. For this reason, you may find it easier to extract large paragraph blocks, then use a word processor to perform editing functions, such as spell check or search and replace.

Creating Neon Effects

Purpose

CorelDRAW enables you to perform sophisticated techniques such as neon effect, multiple outlines for outline/inline effect, drop shadows, and lined text. You can achieve a neon effect by using the **B**lend command.

Steps

1. Determine the thickness of the desired "glow," and set the outline for the text to this width.

2. Duplicate the text by pressing the + key.

3. Set the outline of the new object to hairline.

4. Set one outline dark, and one light. Usually, the text with the hairline outline is set to the light color to create the highlight.

5. Set the fill on both to none.

6. Blend the two objects. A blend of 20 steps usually is enough to achieve the desired effect.

Creating Multiple Outlines for Outline/Inline Effect

Purpose

An outline is a line that goes around the outside of the text. Outlines are used frequently in logos, for example.

Steps

1. To make an outline, you need two copies of the original text.

2. Give the first copy a white outline, equal to twice the thickness of the "gap" desired between the type and the outline.

3. Give the second copy a black outline. The thickness must be the white outline thickness plus twice the thickness of the desired outline.

4. Put the black outline on the bottom, the white outline in the middle, and the original lettering on top.

5. Add more layers for multiple outlines.

 You may get "spikes" on some letters that have very thick outlines. To eliminate this problem, increase the Miter Limit under the <u>S</u>pecial menu (see Chapter 1).

Creating Drop Shadows

The nudge function can be used to quickly make drop shadows. Simply highlight the text, type Ctrl-D to duplicate, nudge to the side and down, change the color, and send back one layer.

Duplicate, then nudge with the arrow keys; send back one layer

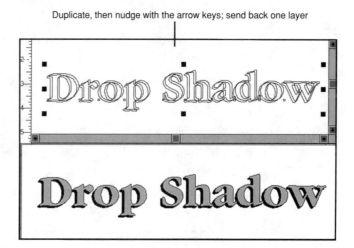

Creating Lined Text (PostScript)

Steps

1. Fill the text with a Spot color.

2. Select PostScript from the Fill menu.

3. Set the halftone screen to Line for lined text.

4. Use the Frequency setting to control the thickness of the lines. A frequency of 10 gives you 10 lines to the inch. (This value is independent of type size, therefore, you must change it if you resize the type.)

5. Set the angle to 0 degrees for horizontal lines, 90 degrees for vertical.

6. Back in the Fill menu, set the Tint to something less than 100%. The less the tint, the thinner the lines. If you want the lines to vary in thickness, use a linear or radial fill.

The example has a black outline and white inline to complete the effect. You cannot see this effect on the Preview screen, but it prints out. Like other non-default PostScript patterns, this one prints slowly.

Notes

You must have a PostScript printer to create the Lined Text effect.

Typographic Refinements

Calligraphic Stroke Compensation

Stretched type looks awkward because it is not uniformly distorted. When stretched vertically, for example, the horizontal strokes become fatter than the vertical strokes. Type designers redraw characters to compensate for this distortion. You can use a calligraphic stroke for the outline to compensate for this distortion. If type is stretched vertically, for example, add a stroke that is stretched to about 200%. This thickens the horizontal dimension, without adding measurably to the vertical dimension. You may want to increase intercharacter spacing to allow for the thickness of the strokes.

 Do not set the thickness of the stroke to less than 1%. A setting lower than this can cause unpredictable results.

Weight Compensation for Large Initial Caps

A large initial cap can look too bold when compared to the smaller type. To solve this problem, use a lighter weight for the large character, or, if the large type is a separate object, add a white outline to "thin" the character.

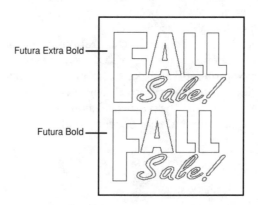

Futura Extra Bold —

Futura Bold —

Special Characters

To access special characters, press the ALT key and type the 4-digit character number shown on the CorelDRAW Character Reference Chart. You can create a card in the Windows Cardfile for frequently used characters, and cut and paste the characters instead of looking up the numbers each time you use them. Some useful special characters are listed below:

- True quotes—characters 0133 and 0134. These should be used instead of the " key.

- Register mark and copyright—characters 0174 and 0169.

- Trademark—character 0147. Use this character instead of typing T and M then shrinking and repositioning them.

- Ligatures—Use the fi (0137) and fl (0138) ligatures for professional-looking type, especially in headlines. (Not all faces contain these characters.)

- Registration mark—character 0184 in the Geographic font. When you work with process color, set the fill for this mark to 100% of all 4 process colors so that it prints on all film layers.

- Square bullet—the lowercase n in Zapf Dingbats. Use this in place of the round bullet (0183) for a more professional look.

  Other useful characters include the degree symbol ° (0176), and the cent sign ¢ (0162).

Using WFN BOSS: Typeface Conversion and Creation

Corel's WFN BOSS utility enables you to convert typefaces from other manufacturers to be used by CorelDRAW, and to export CorelDRAW typefaces for use by other programs. In addition, the CorelDRAW Symbol and Typeface Export Filter enables you to modify existing CorelDRAW typefaces, or even create entirely new typefaces.

In Windows, double-click on the WFN BOSS icon in the CorelDRAW program group. (This group is automatically created when you install CorelDRAW.)

The WFN BOSS menu appears. The following options are available on this menu:

- **Conversion Type.** This menu lists all the available conversion formats. You can make CorelDRAW-compatible fonts from Adobe Type 1, Agfa Compugraphic, Bitstream, DigiFont, Readable PostScript, and Z-Soft Type Foundry fonts, or other fonts that follow these formats. You can also convert CorelDRAW fonts to Adobe Type 1 and Type Foundry formats. Use the arrows to scroll through the listing, and select the desired conversion type.

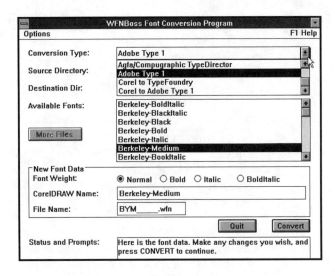

- **Source Directory.** This field lists the source directory for the fonts to convert. To select a new source directory, click on the New Dir button. WFN BOSS works quickly for most typefaces. Therefore, you can convert directly from a floppy disk if you want.

- **Destination Directory.** The Destination Directory receives the converted files. When you create CorelDRAW fonts, this is the directory that stores the CorelDRAW fonts, usually \CORELDRW. When you export fonts, the directory must be the one used by existing fonts of the same format, such as \PSFONTS for Adobe PostScript fonts used by Ventura.

- **Available Fonts.** This window lists the fonts available for conversion. The window only holds 32 fonts at a time. If more than 32 fonts are in a directory, you must use the More Fonts button to access additional fonts. Click on a font name to select a font to convert.

- **New Font Data.** In this window WFN BOSS assigns a the Font Weight and CorelDRAW name to the new font. You can modify these, but unless you are merging fonts (see below), you do not need to change these settings.

Font names can be no more than 25 characters long, with no spaces. In addition, CorelDRAW sets an absolute limit of 256 typefaces and a total of 4000 characters for typeface names. Therefore, keep names as short as possible.

- **Convert.** Click on the Convert button to convert a typeface. The Status and Prompts box gives you progress reports as the conversion proceeds. When the conversion is finished, you can quit WFN BOSS, open CorelDRAW, and use the newly created typeface.

If CorelDRAW is open while you convert typefaces in WFN BOSS, you must restart CorelDRAW to use the new fonts, because the fonts load at startup.

Options

The Options menu gives you a number of options to adjust when you convert typefaces.

- **Font File Info.** Font File Info shows the type family name, PostScript font name and file name, and the number of typestyles in the CorelDRAW font. This helps you locate fonts that have obscure DOS file names, such as BYM_____.WFN (Berkeley Medium).

- **Autoinstall.** When you select Autoinstall, fonts are automatically placed in your CorelDRAW fonts directory. When Autoinstall is disabled, you can put the fonts in any directory you want.

- **Compress Fonts.** Compress Fonts creates the most compact version of the font possible. Compress Fonts can only be used for certain font types, such as Agfa Compugraphic and DigiFont. Refer to the WFN BOSS manual for information about specific font types.

- **Reinstall Fonts.** When you reinstall or update versions of CorelDRAW, CORELDRW.INI is re-written. This wipes out the information on any converted fonts you installed previously. Reinstall Fonts automatically reinstalls all previously converted fonts.

Make sure that you copy the CORELDRW.INI file before you reinstall or update CorelDRAW, so that you have a record of any special changes you made to the file (see Chapters 1 and 17).

- **Convert All.** The Convert All options converts all the fonts on the list automatically. Similar fonts are not merged, however, so do not use this feature except for Bitstream fonts (which are automatically merged).

- **Set Kern.** You normally do not need to adjust this parameter. WFN BOSS sets a default kerning value, based on the font characteristics. If you do need to adjust this value, refer to the WFN BOSS manual for guidance.

Merging Fonts

You can merge up to four different typestyles into a type family. Usually, this means you can have regular, italic, bold, and bold-italic typestyles in a single font. Give each typestyle in the family the same CorelDRAW name, such as Bodoni, and make sure that the file name is the same as well. WFN BOSS adds all four styles into the same file. The advantage of this approach is that you need only one font name in the font listing for the four styles.

If you want to convert a type family that has more than four styles, you must sort them into groups of four.

If you want to exchange files that use converted fonts with another CorelDRAW user, the other person must have the same fonts with the same file names as yours.

Conversions

To convert typefaces in WFN BOSS is easy. Because the various font formats are different, however, each conversion has some special features. The WFN BOSS manual details each conversion. Read the applicable section(s) before you convert fonts, and make backup copies of the fonts you want to convert, just in case something goes wrong.

Exporting CorelDRAW Typefaces

Purpose

You can export CorelDRAW typefaces to Adobe Type 1 and TypeFoundry .OTL formats. This gives you the opportunity to use CorelDRAW typefaces in other programs that support Adobe Type 1 fonts, such as Ventura (GEM version), PageMaker, and other Windows programs, via Adobe Type

Manager. For Ventura, you must convert the Type 1 fonts by using the AFMTOVFM and VFMTOWID utilities that come with Ventura. This is a cumbersome process, so follow the instructions in the WFN BOSS manual carefully.

When you convert CorelDRAW fonts to TypeFoundry's .OTL format, you can use that program to edit the fonts and modify the kerning data. You can even use a CorelDRAW font as the starting point for an entirely new typeface.

Use WFN BOSS as a typeface translator, to convert Bitstream and other formats to Adobe Type 1, or vice versa.

Metamorphosis, by Altsys, is a Mac program that converts Mac fonts to PC-type Adobe Type 1 fonts, and vice versa. You can, therefore, import Mac fonts into CorelDRAW, or CorelDRAW fonts into the Mac environment where they can be modified by Fontgrapher (another Altsys program).

Converting Symbol Fonts to Type Fonts

Purpose

Some of the CorelDRAW Symbol fonts can be converted to type fonts via WFN BOSS. To do this, you must export the Symbol font to Adobe Type 1 or TypeFoundry format, and then import it back into CorelDRAW font format. This adds the Symbol font to your typeface list, and makes it possible for you to access the symbols as type. Therefore, you can use Fit Text to Path and other type-based functions on symbols.

Steps

1. Select the Symbol font from the CorelDRAW directory, and Export to either Adobe or TypeFoundry formats.

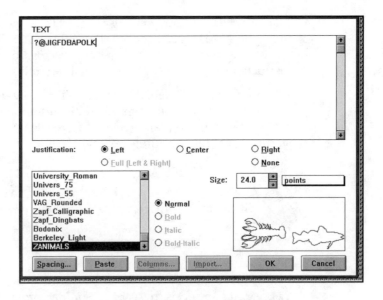

2. Import the font into CorelDRAW format. (Make sure the file name WFN BOSS uses to save the file is different from the Symbol font name, so that the original font is not overwritten.)

3. Open CorelDRAW, and use the new font as you would any type font. (You must print out a character set to see which symbols are assigned to which keys.)

Some symbol fonts contain complex symbols which may not convert successfully. You can use the CorelDRAW Symbol and Typeface Export function (see below) to delete those characters that do not convert successfully.

WFN BOSS adds the new typefaces you import to the end of the typeface list in the CORELDRW.INI file. If you want the new fonts to appear in alphabetical order along with the existing fonts, you need to edit CORELDRW.INI to reorganize the list.

Exporting CorelDRAW Symbols and Typefaces

Purpose

A powerful feature of the CorelDRAW Export menu is the ability to export CorelDRAW objects to CorelDRAW fonts. This gives you the capability to modify or add characters to a font, add symbols to a font, or even design an entire typeface. The following example adds the ffl ligature to a CorelDRAW typeface.

Steps

1. Create the ffl ligature. Start with the existing fl ligature—character 0138—and a second f. Convert these to curves and combine into a single object. Work at a large size, in this case 720 points, so that the characters are as smooth as possible. The final object must be a single curve, with no intersecting points. Set the ruler origin to the bottom left hand corner of the character.

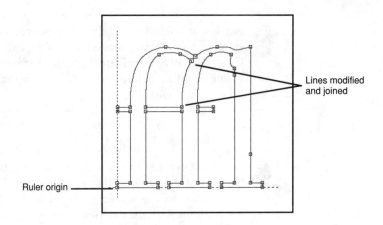

Lines modified and joined

Ruler origin

2. Select CorelDRAW Symbol and Typeface from the Export menu. If more than one object is in your CorelDRAW file, make sure that you select only one object to export, and check **S**elected Objects Only. The Export CorelDRAW Symbol menu appears.

3. Select a typeface to export to, and click OK. The Typeface Information menu appears.

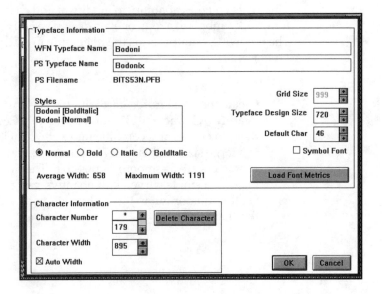

Backup the target font file before you export to it. That way, if something goes wrong, you do not have to reinstall CorelDRAW to restore the font.

Unless you are creating a new font, you do not need to change the WFN Typeface or PS Typeface names. Make sure that the correct typestyle (regular, bold, etc.) is selected.

4. Enter the point size of the character you are exporting. (In this case it is 720 points.)

5. Enter the character number to export to. Unused characters appear in gray. Export the ffl ligature to a seldom used character, such as number 179. (Do not use character numbers below 33.) Unless you are creating a new typeface, you do not need to alter any other settings.

6. Click on OK to export the new character.

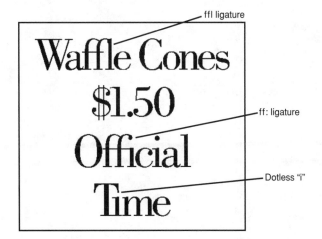

 To simplify your work, add frequently used symbols to a typeface. The triangle, for example, can be added to a typeface to be used as a bullet. It is otherwise available only as a Zapf Dingbat (Dixieland) that must be rotated. When you add it to a font, however, you can automatically align it with the other type.

Creating Custom Typefaces

Purpose

You can use the CorelDRAW Symbol and Typeface Export function to create entire typefaces. This is a complex process, however. The WFN BOSS manual contains a detailed description of the steps you must perform to create a typeface.

CHAPTER 5

Moving and Transforming Objects

Creating an object is just the beginning in constructing a good piece of art. You probably will want to move or transform the object to create the effect you want. After you master these simple skills, you can create professional-looking artwork.

In this chapter, you learn the following operations:

- Moving objects by using the menu method
- Moving objects by using the nudge method
- Stretching objects
- Using Rotate and Skew mode
- Clearing transformations

Moving Objects with the Mouse

Purpose

You can move an object or objects so that you can place them in a new location.

Steps

1. Select the Pick tool.

2. Click on the wireframe of the object or objects you want to move.

3. Press and hold down the mouse button and drag the object to the new location. The cursor changes to an arrowheaded cross, and a highlighting box appears. If you stop dragging the object, the object is redrawn.

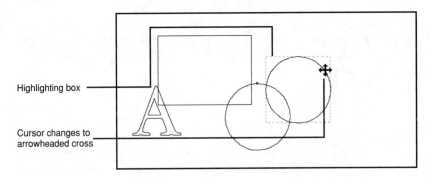

Highlighting box

Cursor changes to
arrowheaded cross

4. When the object is in the desired position, release the mouse button.

Notes

You can continue to move the object as long as you hold down the mouse button.

With a little practice, you can select and move an object in the same operation.

 If you are moving a complex object, redraw can take a long time. Keep the highlighting box moving to avoid the redraw. With Version 2.01 and above, you can disable the redrawing function.

To move multiple objects, use the Shift key or marquee to select them, then move the objects as a single group. Group multiple objects together (Alt-G) so that you can move all objects at once. If you miss an object, select it immediately after the move operation and press Ctrl-R.

Press and hold down the Control key as you drag an object to constrain the movement to horizontal and vertical directions.

If you want to leave a copy of the object that you are moving in the original position, press the plus (+) key on the numeric keypad. The copy is layered underneath the original, unlike the **D**uplicate command, which places a copy on top of the original. The keyboard shortcut for this operation (in Version 2.01) is the right mouse button.

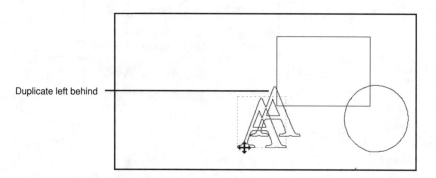

Duplicate left behind

Using the Menu Method To Move Objects

Purpose

This task teaches you to use the **T**ransform menu to move an object.

Steps

1. Select the object or group of objects you want to move with the Pick tool.

2. From the **T**ransform menu, select **M**ove. The **M**ove dialog box appears.

3. Enter the **H**orizontal and **V**ertical distance you want to move the object. Entering negative numbers moves the object down and left; positive numbers move the object up and right. You can change the unit of measure by clicking on the unit names.

4. Select <u>L</u>eave Original to leave a copy of the object behind.

5. Select <u>A</u>bsolute Coordinates if you want the move to be made relative to the ruler origins. Highlight which part of the object to place on the specified coordinates when the diagram appears.

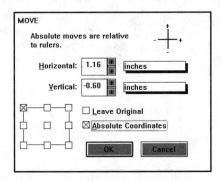

6. Click OK.

Notes

If you select a new object after you make a menu move, you can move the new object the same distance by pressing Ctrl-R.

The shortcut key for the <u>M</u>ove command is Ctrl-L.

 To move an object to a new location by using absolute coordinates, drag the ruler lines to the desired position, then enter a 0 value for both the <u>H</u>orizontal and <u>V</u>ertical coordinates in the <u>M</u>ove dialog box.

Moving Objects with <u>N</u>udge

Purpose

You can move an object or group of objects by "nudging" it in the direction of the arrow key you press. This method can be useful for precision alignments and offsets.

Steps

1. Select the object or objects you want to move.

2. From the **S**pecial menu, select Pr**e**ferences. The Pr**e**ferences dialog box appears.

3. Enter the maximum value that you want the object to move. (For more information on **N**udge, see Chapter 1.)

4. Press the arrow key that points in the direction that you want to move the object or group of objects.

Notes

Set the minimum nudge value at .1 point to precisely align objects. A larger value of .5 or 1 is useful for making adjustments without zooming in.

To make the move continuous, press and hold down the arrow key.

 To temporarily set a nudge value that is different from the preset value, use the menu method to move the object by the desired nudge value. You then can nudge the object repeatedly by using the **R**epeat (Ctrl-R) command or by pressing the arrow keys.

Stretching Objects with the Mouse

Purpose

You can change the shape and size of an object by stretching it. CorelDRAW provides two methods you can use to stretch objects.

Steps

1. Select an object or group of objects by clicking with the mouse or drawing a marquee.

2. Click on one of the eight control nodes and drag the mouse to stretch the object. The side nodes stretch the object horizontally and vertically. The corner nodes scale the object uniformly so that the object retains its proportions.

3. Release the mouse button when the object appears as you want.

Notes

Press and hold down the Control key as you stretch an object to stretch in increments of 100 percent.

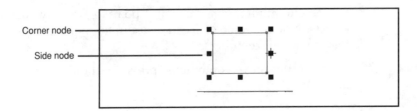

Corner node
Side node

 You can use the constrained stretch (Ctrl-drag) to temporarily flip an object or group of objects to get them out of the way. This process is much like lifting an overlay. To shift the objects back into place, just repeat the constrained stretch.

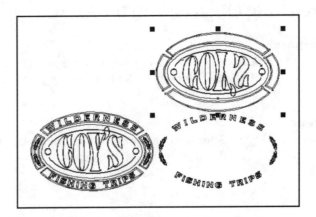

If you press the plus (+) key on the numeric keypad as you stretch an object, a copy of the original object is left behind. Press Ctrl-+ to create a mirror image of the object.

The Status Line displays the amount an object is being stretched or scaled. A negative number indicates a reflection, or mirror image.

```
orm   Effects  Arrange  Display  Special
                      scale:  205.4 %
      Width:6,8   Height:4,6   Center:(4,5, -19,10) picas, points
```

 You cannot shrink objects to less than one percent or more than 3000 percent. You can, by repeatedly shrinking, set the dimensions of an object to zero. When this happens, you no longer can size the object in the dimension(s) that have a zero value.

Press and hold down the Shift key to uniformly stretch or size an object. The object grows from its center.

Using the Menu Method To Stretch Objects

Purpose

If you know the percentage that you want to stretch or scale an object, you can use the Transform menu.

Steps

1. Select the object or group of objects you want to stretch.

2. From the Transform menu, select Stretch & Mirror. The Stretch & Mirror dialog box appears.

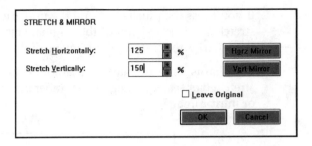

3. Enter the percentages that you want to stretch the object horizontally and vertically. You also can click the arrows beside the boxes to set the percentages.

4. Choose Leave Original to leave a copy of the object in its original location.

5. Choose the Horizontal or Vertical button to indicate which way to flip the object.

6. Click OK.

Notes

The shortcut key for Stretch & Mirror is Ctrl-Q.

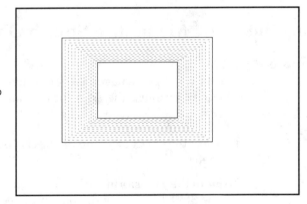

Use Stretch & Mirror to create nudged effect.

You can stretch or scale an object incrementally by creating the equivalent of a nudge effect with the Stretch & Mirror dialog box. Enter a small horizontal or vertical value, such as from one to five percent. Then use the Repeat (Ctrl-R) to nudge the object to the desired size.

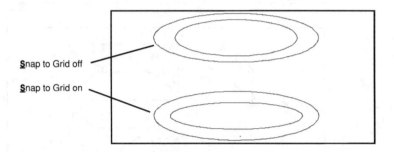

Snap to Grid off

Snap to Grid on

If you draw a larger oval or rectangle around a smaller oval or rectangle, the space between the two lines is not uniform. The less square the objects are, the greater the difference. The percentage increase in the long axis is greater in absolute terms than a similar percentage increase in the short axis.

To keep the space uniform, increase the long axis less than the short axis. Alternately, turn on Snap to Grid and set the grid increment to the desired spacing.

To mirror an object, scale the object by a negative amount. Drag one of the control points to the opposite side of the object as you press and hold the Control key. To place a mirror image in exactly the same position as the original, press Ctrl-Shift. This method is faster than Stretch & Mirror.

If you want to create complex symmetrical objects, create half the object and then create a mirror of the object. Then combine both elements. Designs that are bilaterally symmetrical are even easier to create. Just create one-quarter of the object and then perform a mirror twice. (See Chapter 6 for information on the Combine command.)

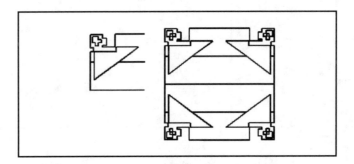

Entering Rotate and Skew Mode

Purpose

You can rotate or skew objects by entering the Rotate and Skew mode.

Steps

1. Select the Pick tool.

2. Double-click on the object or group of objects you want to rotate and skew. The control handles change to arrows. A circle with a dot in it appears in the center of the object or objects. This circle is the center of rotation.

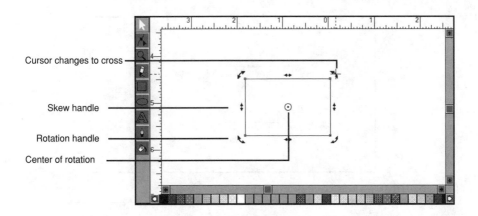

Cursor changes to cross

Skew handle

Rotation handle

Center of rotation

Rotating an Object with the Mouse

Purpose

This task teaches you to rotate an object or objects. The object rotates around the center of rotation.

Steps

1. Enter Rotate & Skew mode by double-clicking on the object or objects you want to rotate, as discussed in the preceding section.

2. Position the cursor on one of the curved corner arrows. The cursor changes to a cross when it is positioned correctly.

3. Press and hold down the mouse button as you drag the object.

Notes

Hold down the Control key to constrain the rotation in 15-degree increments. This value is set in the Preferences dialog box in the Special menu.

Pressing the plus (+) key on the numeric keypad as you rotate an object causes CorelDRAW to leave a copy of the rotated object behind.

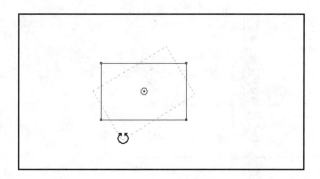

 You can move the center of rotation. Click on the rotation circle and drag it to the new location. If you hold down the Control key as you move the center of rotation, the center snaps to one of eight control nodes for the object.

Use the **R**epeat (Ctrl-R) command to rotate the object by the same increment as the last rotation performed.

If you select a new object after repeating a rotation, the new object rotates around the *first* object's center of rotation.

 If you rotate an object repeatedly, its position may wander slightly due to cumulative mathematical errors. You may need to use the nudge keys to move the object into its correct position.

Using the Menu Method To Rotate Objects

Purpose

This task teaches you to use the menu method when rotating an object or group of objects.

Steps

1. Select the Pick tool.

2. From the <u>T</u>ransform menu, select <u>R</u>otate & Skew.

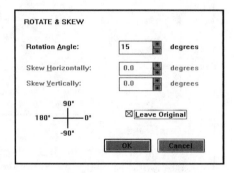

3. Specify the Rotation <u>A</u>ngle in degrees.

4. If you choose <u>L</u>eave Original, a copy of the object is rotated.

Notes

You can rotate objects in tenth-degree increments. Finer increments, such as .157 degrees, are rounded down to the nearest tenth.

The shortcut key for <u>R</u>otate and Skew is Ctrl-N.

Using Multiple Rotations

You can create complex drawings by using the rotation method. Suppose that you want to create a drawing of a bicycle wheel. The drawing is not nearly as complex if you use the rotation method.

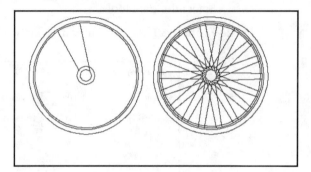

Create a circle for the hub of the wheel. Duplicate (Ctrl-N) and scale up the circle to complete the hub. To form the tire, duplicate the circle again and scale up the duplicates with the Shift key to keep them centered on the hub. Now draw a single set of spokes. Shift the center of rotation to the lower right corner. Duplicate and rotate the spokes with the plus (+) key. Press Ctrl-R until you form a complete wheel.

Skewing Objects with the Mouse

Purpose

CorelDRAW enables you to *skew*, or slant, an object or a group of objects. You can use the mouse to skew an object, as discussed in this section, or you can use the **T**ransform menu. The menu method is discussed in the next section.

Steps

1. Select the object or objects you want to skew.

2. Click a second time on the outline of the object or objects.

3. Drag the skew handles (the horizontal and vertical arrows) to skew the object.

Skew handle ———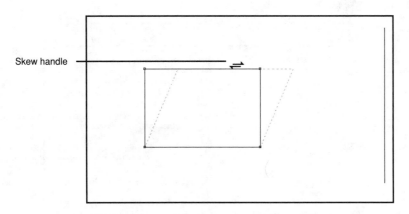

Using the Menu Method To Skew Objects

Purpose

CorelDRAW also enables you to skew an object or group of objects using the Transform menu.

Steps

1. Select the object or objects you want to skew.

2. From the Transform menu, select Rotate & Skew. The Rotate & Skew dialog box appears.

3. Enter the amount in degrees that you want to skew the object. You also can click the arrows to select a skew value.

Notes

You can constrain the skew motion by pressing and holding down the Control key as you drag the mouse. The object is skewed in 15-degree increments or as specified in the Preferences dialog box.

Press and hold the plus (+) key as you drag the mouse to leave a copy of the original object behind.

The keyboard shortcut for Rotate & Skew is Ctrl-N.

You also can skew objects to create shadows for specific objects.

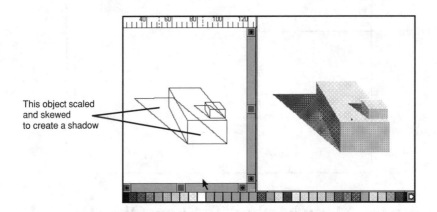

This object scaled and skewed to create a shadow

Clearing Transformations

Purpose

You can undo any rotation, skewing, and sizing that you performed on an object.

Steps

1. Select the Pick tool.

2. Select the object or objects.

3. From the Transform menu, choose Clear
    Transformations.

Notes

If you convert an object to curves, the Clear Transformation
command no longer removes any previous transformations.
(See Chapter 6 for more information on converting objects to
curves.)

CHAPTER **6**

Arranging and Aligning Objects

You can use many of CorelDRAW's special features to add depth and interest to your drawings. Using layers to show dimension or grouping objects together to form a new perspective can be quite effective visually.

In this chapter, you learn to use commands from the **A**rrange menu to group and manipulate objects in your drawings. The tasks discussed include the following:

- Grouping and ungrouping objects
- Combining objects
- Creating clipping masks
- Breaking objects apart (Uncombine)
- Converting objects and text to curves
- Manipulating layers
- Aligning objects

```
Arrange
To Front      ShiftPgUp
To Back       ShiftPgDn
Forward One   PgUp
Back One      PgDn
Reverse Order

Group         ^G
Ungroup       ^U

Combine       ^C
Break Apart   ^K

Convert To Curves ^V

Align...      ^A
Fit Text To Path  ^F
Align To Baseline ^Z
Straighten Text
```

Grouping Objects

Purpose

Grouping objects makes it easier to maintain the relationships of objects that make up a complex element.

Steps

1. Select the objects to be grouped by shift-clicking with the Pick tool or dragging a marquee.

2. Select **G**roup from the **A**rrange menu. The grouped objects can now be moved and transformed as a unit. When the group is selected, the highlighting box surrounds the entire group. The status line reads Group of x objects, indicating the group is selected.

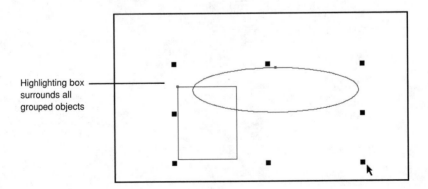

Highlighting box
surrounds all
grouped objects

To group everything in the drawing, use Select <u>A</u>ll from the Edit menu; then group the objects.

Notes

You cannot edit nodes of grouped objects or blend or extrude grouped objects.

You can combine groups of objects into larger groups up to 10 levels deep.

The keyboard shortcut for grouping objects is Ctrl-G.

Ungrouping Grouped Objects

Purpose

You can ungroup objects you previously grouped earlier after you manipulate or change the group.

Steps

1. Select the group.

2. Choose <u>U</u>ngroup from the <u>A</u>rrange menu. The objects are ungrouped; each of the individual objects are highlighted. The status bar reads x objects selected.

Notes

The <u>U</u>ngroup command works on only one level at a time. You must ungroup each grouping separately.

The keyboard shortcut for ungrouping objects is Ctrl-U.

To quickly remove an object from a group, follow the preceding steps, and then Shift-click on the object or objects you want to exclude. Then press Ctrl-G (<u>G</u>roup) to regroup the objects.

Combining Objects

Purpose

Unlike Group, Combine changes two or more objects into a single object, converting text objects, rectangles, and ellipses to curves. The combined object has the fill and outline of the first object created.

Steps

1. Select the objects to be combined.

2. Select Combine from the Arrange menu.

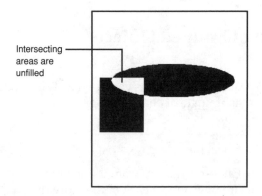

Intersecting areas are unfilled

 Use Combine to create special effects with type. Note that type is converted to curves by the Combine command.

Notes

Grouped objects cannot be combined. They must first be ungrouped.

The keyboard shortcut to combine objects is Ctrl-C.

Creating Clipping Masks

Purpose

A mask creates a border around an object or group of objects, masking off any unwanted parts of your drawing.

Steps

1. Create the desired frame shape.

2. Draw a larger masking shape that encloses all the objects to be masked.

3. Combine the frame shape and the masking shape.

4. Use To _F_ront to put the clipping mask on top of the other objects.

5. Set the fill to White and outline to None (unless you want a printing border around the objects).

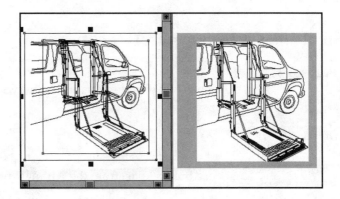

Notes

Whether you should group or combine objects depends on the situation:

• If you want to preserve the outline and fill of the original objects, use _G_roup.

• If you want to preserve text, rectangles and ellipses, use _G_roup.

- If the objects have the same attributes and are not touching, use <u>C</u>ombine to save memory. Combined objects also draw faster.

- If you want to create a clipping mask, use <u>C</u>ombine.

- If you want to edit the nodes of different curve objects at once, use <u>C</u>ombine.

- If you want to join two separate curve segments, use <u>C</u>ombine.

CorelDRAW has a limit of about 2000 nodes for any single object. Objects with more than 1000 nodes may cause trouble with printing or previewing. Break apart any objects with more than a few hundred nodes whenever possible.

Breaking Objects Apart (Uncombine)

Purpose

If an object has two or more separate paths, you can break it apart.

Steps

1. Select the desired object.

2. Choose Brea<u>k</u> Apart from the <u>A</u>rrange menu.

   All the paths in the object are broken into separate objects. The status line reads x `objects selected`.

Note

The keyboard shortcut for Brea<u>k</u> Apart is Ctrl-K.

Converting Objects and Text to Curves

Purpose

Using <u>C</u>ombine to convert text, rectangles and ellipses to curve objects gives the objects new capabilities for manipulation and transformation. Although the objects lose their individual features (text can no longer be edited, for example), as curve objects, individual nodes of the curve can now be manipulated.

By converting text to curves, you can perform many manipulations that would otherwise be impossible. For example, you can use text as a clipping mask to fill the letters with another object.

Text in two colors ———

Text combined with a graphic ———

Text used as a clipping mask ———

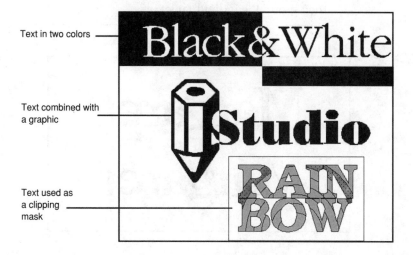

The text in the following figure was converted to curves, the number of points doubled using the **A**dd command, and all segments converted to lines. (See Chapter 4 for more information on converting segments to lines).

If a long text string is converted to curves, the resulting object
can have a large number of nodes. To avoid trouble, break
large text strings into separate objects.

When converted to curves, overlapping letters create
a white space in the overlap. Break the letters apart,
combine multipart characters such as a and e, and
then group the individual letters.

Margaret
Margaret

Think before you convert text to curves. If you can achieve the
desired effect by using E_dit Envelope or Perspecti_ve, you can
retain the editability of your text. Make a copy of your text
before you convert it so that you can start over if you make a
mistake. The copy also preserves a record of the type face,
size, and spacing of the original text.

Compensate for the distortions created from
stretched text by converting to curves and editing
the nodes.

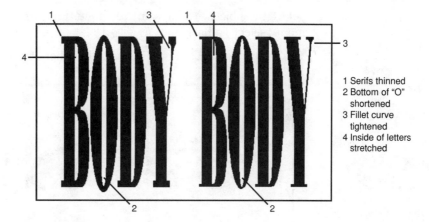

1 Serifs thinned
2 Bottom of "O"
  shortened
3 Fillet curve
  tightened
4 Inside of letters
  stretched

Sending Objects to the Front Layer

Purpose

To <u>F</u>ront places the currently selected object(s) on top of all other objects.

Steps

1. Select the object(s) you want to move.

2. From the <u>A</u>rrange menu, select To <u>F</u>ront.

   The selected object appears on top of all other objects.

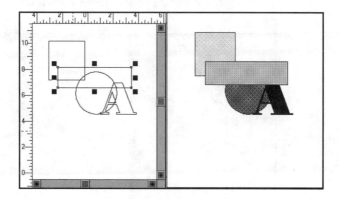

Notes

You also can place the currently selected object(s) beneath all other objects.

Select the object(s) you want to move. From the **A**rrange menu, select To **B**ack.

The selected object appears beneath the other objects.

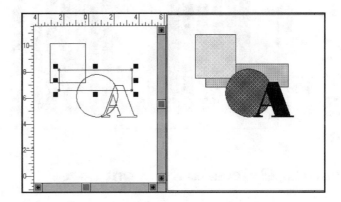

Sending Objects to the Next Layer Forward

Purpose

You can move the selected object(s) up one layer in position.

Steps

1. Select the object(s) you want to move.

2. From the **A**rrange menu, select Forward **O**ne.

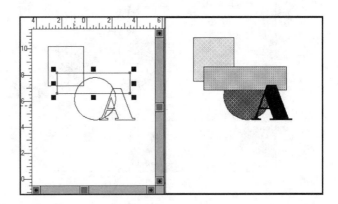

Sending Objects to the Next Layer Back

Purpose

You can move the selected object(s) back one layer in position.

Steps

1. Select the object(s) you want to move.

2. From the <u>A</u>rrange menu, select Back O<u>n</u>e.

Reversing the Order

Purpose

You can reverse the order of the selected objects.

Steps

1. Select the object(s) you want to reverse.

2. From the <u>A</u>rrange menu, select <u>R</u>everse Order.

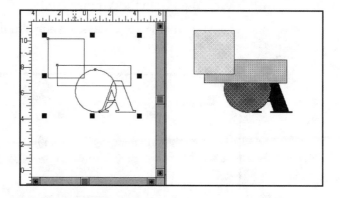

 You can see the way in which objects are layered in the drawing by pressing the Tab and Shift-Tab key combinations to move forward or backward through the stack of objects.

Notes

You can use the following keyboard shortcuts to move among the layers of a drawing:

Shift-PgUp   Moves selected object to the front

Shift-PgDn   Moves selected object to the back

PgUp   Moves selected object forward one layer

PgDn   Moves selected object back one layer

Aligning Objects

Purpose

This option enables you to precisely align the currently selected objects.

Steps

1. Select the object you want to align.

2. Select **A**lign from the **A**rrange menu.

   The **A**lign dialog box shows the effect of the various alignment options.

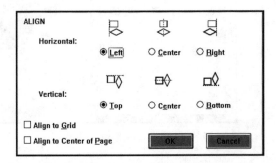

3. Select the type of alignment you want.

4. Click on OK.

Notes

As you align objects, the last object selected maintains its position; all other objects move to align with this object. If you use the marquee-select technique, the first object created is the object that remains in place. If you cannot remember the creation order, select the object to align after you select all the other objects.

The keyboard shortcut for **A**lign is Ctrl-A.

The Align to **G**rid option aligns the selected objects to the nearest grid marker. You can align a single object to the grid. The horizontal and vertical settings determine how the objects align to the grid.

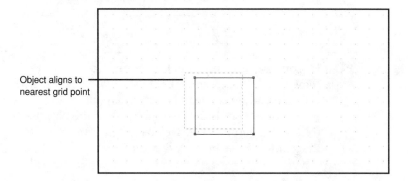

Object aligns to nearest grid point

The Align to Center of **P**age option aligns objects according to the horizontal and vertical settings, and then aligns the objects as a group relative to the center of the page. You can align a single object to the center of the page. If this option is selected, horizontal center and vertical center alignment are automatically selected. You can override these settings by clicking on others. You can disable one of the settings by clicking on it.

 The **R**epeat command (Ctrl-R) repeats the alignment operation, even if different objects are selected.

 If you are aligning text strings, CorelDRAW remembers the descender height as it calculates size. This calculation can lead to misalignments with the **A**lign command. Either manually align the objects (**N**udge is useful for precise positioning), or convert the text to curves before aligning.

CHAPTER **7**

Using Outlines and Fills

Every object within CorelDRAW, including a text string, has an outline and a fill. You can make extensive modifications to both of these attributes.

The *outline* of an object is the border that defines its edges. An outline has a shape, or *width*, and color or *shading*. An object's outline may be a solid, thin black line, a thick, patterned dashed line, or any number of other designs.

The *fill* of an object is its interior, the space inside the outline. A fill may be empty, or it may be a colored or gray-shaded pattern.

This chapter teaches you to modify the outline and fill of an object to add texture, dimension and other creative effects to your drawing. You will learn the following techniques:

- Setting and editing outline width and shading
- Selecting and creating arrowheads
- Using the Fill tool
- Using and creating bit-map and vector pattern fills
- Using and creating linear and radial fountain fills
- Using the color palette to assign spot or process color
- Setting the default Fill and Outline settings
- Copying Outline and Fill styles
- Trapping colors

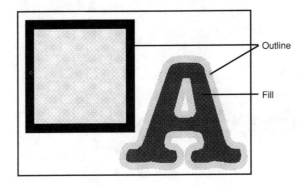

Setting Outline Width and Shading

Purpose

This task teaches you to set the Outline and Color attributes for an object.

Steps

1. Select the object you want to change.

2. Select the Outline tool. A flyout menu appears. This menu contains two rows of icons: the top row selections determine the shape or width of the outline; the second row of icons determine color or shade of gray.

3. Choose one of the following options that customize the width of the outline pen:

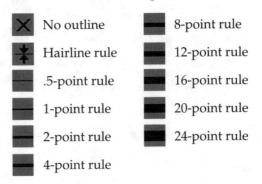

No outline		8-point rule	
Hairline rule		12-point rule	
.5-point rule		16-point rule	
1-point rule		20-point rule	
2-point rule		24-point rule	
4-point rule			

Choose one of the following options that customize the color or shading of the outline pen:

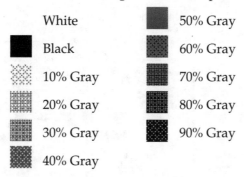

	White		50% Gray
	Black		60% Gray
	10% Gray		70% Gray
	20% Gray		80% Gray
	30% Gray		90% Gray
	40% Gray		

Notes

If you plan to reproduce a hairline rule from high-resolution (greater than 300 dpi) images, use the dialog box described in the following section to specify at least .25 points to ensure that your hairlines reproduce clearly.

Editing Outline Width

Purpose

This task teaches you to customize the width and stroke of the Outline pen.

Steps

1. Select the object whose outline you want to edit.

2. Select the Outline tool. The Outline flyout menu appears.

3. Select the Pen icon. The Outline Pen dialog box appears.

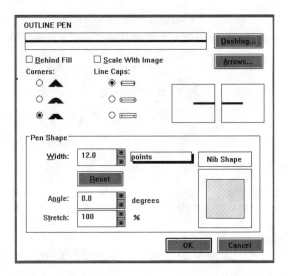

4. Select **D**ashing... if you want to choose from a variety of dotted lines. Click on the pattern you want to use.

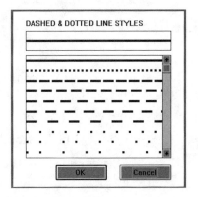

5. Select **B**ehind Fill to put the fill on top of the object's outline. In the default settings, the outline thickness is centered on the outline and sits in front of the fill. Select **B**ehind Fill to put the fill in front of the inner half of the outline. With an 8-point outline, for example, only the outer 4 points of the outline show. See the figure accompanying this task's notes to see the difference between the default fill and **B**ehind Fill.

6. Select **S**cale With Image so that the outline thickness is scaled proportionately as you change the size of an object.

7. Select the corner type that you want to use. You can choose Miter, Round, or Bevel.

    *   **Mitered** corners cause the edges of the lines to extend until they meet. The corner point can extend far beyond the actual line if you are working with extremely small angles. You can set a miter limit from the **P**rint Preview box under Preferences in the **S**pecial menu. CorelDRAW can be set to miter all corners with angles less than 5° up to 45°.

    *   **Rounded** corners draw the outer edge of the corner as an arc. The inside of the corner is not rounded.

    *   **Beveled** corners appear beveled at the outside corners, as if the miter limit were zero.

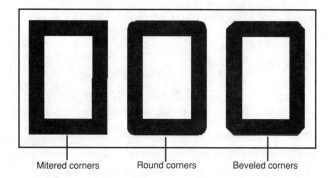

Mitered corners   Round corners   Beveled corners

8. Select the Line Cap option you want to use. You can choose from the following options:

    *   **Butt** caps are squared off at the end point.

    *   **Round** caps create a rounded end point.

    *   **Square** caps create a squared-off end, but extend half the thickness of the line width past each end point.

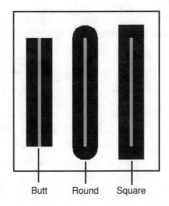

Butt   Round   Square

9. Set the width of the pen stroke in the **W**idth box. You can enter a number or click the arrows to select a setting. You can choose from Inches, Centimeters, Picas and Points, and Fractional Points.

10. Select the A**n**gle and S**t**retch of your pen.

   • S**t**retch changes the nib shape from the default square or circle to a thinner shape. Use this option to create calligraphic effects.

   • A**n**gle rotates the nib's orientation so that you can modify the calligraphic effect.

   In this example, the top line shows a 10% stretch and a 0-degree angle; the second line shows a 10% stretch and a 45-degree angle; and the last line shows a 10% stretch and a 90-degree angle.

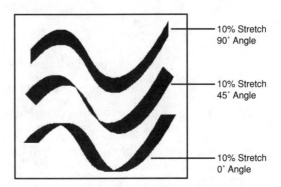

10% Stretch
90° Angle

10% Stretch
45° Angle

10% Stretch
0° Angle

11. Click OK.

Notes

Use **B**ehind Fill on characters with a relatively thick outline to keep the outline from distorting the characters.

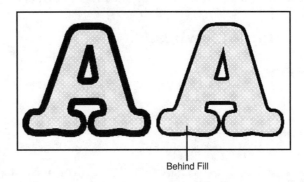

Behind Fill

If you choose **S**cale With Image, the thickness of the outline changes based on the original size of the object. Thus, the actual thickness of the rule may not match the preset thickness. For example, enlarging an object thickens the outline.

 To prevent the outline of an object from becoming distorted, apply the outline value after you make transformations.

Create your own dash patterns by editing the CORELDRW.DOT file. Open the file in a text editor such as Windows Notepad and follow the on-screen instructions, or consult the *CorelDRAW! Technical Reference* manual for details. You can define up to 40 dash styles in one file.

 Do not set the **S**tretch option to an extremely low value (below 5%). You might experience unpredictable results, especially with older versions of the PostScript language.

The **R**eset button sets the Outline A**n**gle to 0 degrees and the St**r**etch to 100%. If **S**cale With Image is selected, **R**eset may not have an effect on the outline.

Pen controls have no effect on bit maps, with one exception. Setting the outline to none makes the bit map nonprinting, and it does not appear in the Preview. Use this option to temporarily turn off the bit map display.

Selecting Arrowheads

Purpose

You can end your lines with a variety of arrowheads and other symbols.

Steps

1. Select the object whose outline you want to edit.

2. Select the Outline tool. A flyout menu appears.

3. Select the Pen icon. A dialog box appears.

4. Select the **A**rrows button. The Arrowhead Selection dialog box appears. The symbol in the left box begins the line, and the symbol in the right box ends the line. Alternate symbols appear in the boxed section below.

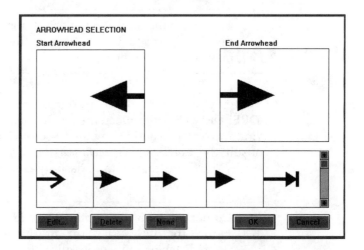

5. Select a Start Arrowhead and End Arrowhead. Press the left mouse button to select the beginning arrowhead, and press the right mouse button to select the ending arrowhead. You can use the up- and down-arrow keys to scroll through the alternate arrowhead selections.

6. Click OK.

Notes

The <u>D</u>elete option removes the selected arrowhead from the listing. The <u>N</u>one option removes the arrowhead from the beginning or end of the line.

You can edit the arrowhead shape and size. Choose <u>E</u>dit in the Arrowhead Selection dialog box to resize and reposition the selected arrowhead symbol.

You can choose the options that appear on the left side of the box to reposition the arrowhead. The <u>4</u>X option magnifies the arrowhead by a factor of 4.

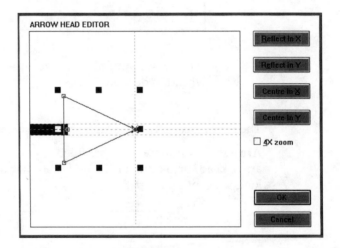

 Editing the arrowhead permanently changes its shape unless you choose Cancel.

Creating Arrowheads

Purpose

If you do not want to use one of the standard arrowhead selections, you can convert any single selected object into an arrowhead.

Steps

1. Select the object you want to use as the arrowhead shape.

2. From the **S**pecial menu, select Create **A**rrow.

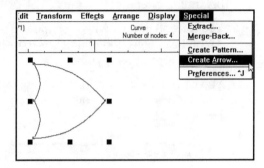

3. Use the Arrowhead Editor to size and position the arrowhead as desired.

Notes

The Arrowhead file has a capacity of 100 arrowheads.

Arrowheads automatically are filled. If you want an outlined arrowhead, break one of the nodes so that the object is no longer a continuous path.

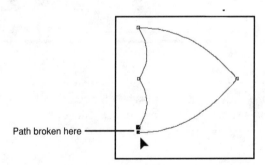

Path broken here

To construct an arrowhead from two or more objects, combine the objects into a single object before you create the arrowhead. For more information on **C**ombine, see Chapter 6.

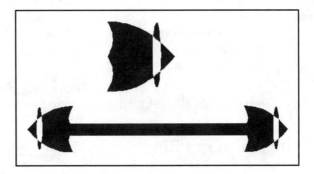

Using the Fill Tool

Purpose

This tool enables you to fill the inner area of an object. You can select the shade, color, and pattern of the fill.

Steps

1. Select the object you want to fill.

2. Click on the Fill tool. A flyout menu appears. The top row of options from left to right include Uniform fill, No fill, White, Black, Bitmap fill, Vector fill, Fountain fill, and PostScript text fill. The bottom row of options provides eight gray fills (10 percent black to 80 percent black).

	Uniform fill		10% Black
	No fill		20% Black
	White		30% Black
	Black		40% Black
	Bitmap fill		50% Black
	Vector fill		60% Black
	Fountain fill		70% Black
	Postscript fill		80% Black

Notes

The currently selected object's fill appears in the Status Line. If you are working with more than one object, the Status Line does not display the fill name.

You must use Preview or print the drawing in order to see the actual effect of the fill, for they do not appear on the workspace.

Selecting Bitmap Fills

Purpose

Bit-map fills are fixed-resolution patterns made from bit-map tiles. The bit-map pattern remains at a fixed size and orientation when the object it fills is scaled or rotated.

Steps

1. Select the Bitmap fill icon. The Bitmap Fill Pattern dialog box appears.

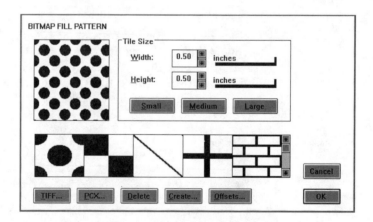

2. Select the bit-map pattern that you want to use by clicking on the desired pattern. The selected pattern appears in the preview box. The visual display at the bottom of the box shows the available bit-map patterns. Use the scroll bars to move through the selections.

3. Set the height and width of the pattern. Three predefined sizes are available: <u>S</u>mall (.25"), <u>M</u>edium (.5"), and <u>L</u>arge (1").

4. To control the way in which tiles line up, click on **O**ffsets. The Tile Offsets dialog box appears. The Starting Tile Offset option enables you to begin the pattern with part of a tile. The Inter Row/Column Offset option enables you to shift the rows or columns of tiles so that they align like bricks.

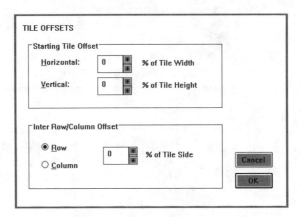

5. Click OK. The Bitmap Pattern Color dialog box appears.

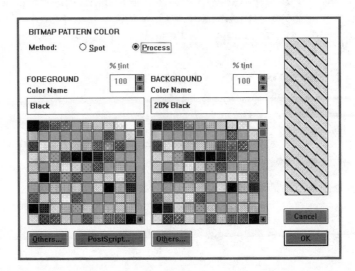

6. Make your color selections for the foreground and the background.

Notes

You can import TIFF and PCX files to use as bit-map fills. CorelDRAW reduces (and possibly distorts) any imported bit map to 256 x 356 bits. Any white space in the file around the image is included in the import.

If you delete the selected pattern from the bit map list, you cannot easily restore the pattern. Objects that were previously filled with a deleted pattern, however, retain that pattern.

Bit-map fills take a long time to print and display. If you are working on a drawing that you must print or preview often, add bit-map fills as a last step in the drawing process.

If you clear the screen in the Pattern Editor by clicking one of the bit-map size options and then click OK, you create a blank bit-map pattern. Only 195 patterns fit in the library; therefore, you may want to delete blank patterns.

Selecting Vector Pattern Fills

Purpose

Vector patterns are CorelDRAW files that you can use as fill patterns. These patterns retain their sharpness when they are resized.

Steps

    1. Select the Vector icon. The Load Vector Pattern dialog box appears.

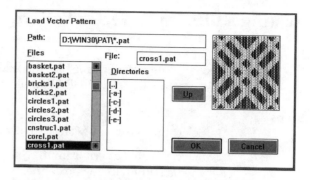

2. Select the vector pattern you want to use and click OK. All vector pattern files have the PAT extension. If you placed the PAT files in their own directory, you may have to change the path.

3. The Vector Fill Pattern dialog box appears. You set the width and height of the pattern here. You can choose Small, Medium, or Large.

4. Select Seamless Tiling to correct the seams that sometimes appear between tiles. The tiles are overlapped slightly.

5. The Offsets option works the same way as the Seamless Tiling option.

6. Click OK.

Notes

Vector patterns remain a fixed size and orientation when you rotate or resize an object.

You can edit vector patterns in CorelDRAW. To open a pattern file, use the Open command and change the CDR extension to PAT. After you edit the pattern, use the Create Pattern command from the Special menu to save the revised pattern under a new file name so that you do not overwrite the existing pattern.

Creating a Bitmap or Vector Pattern

Purpose

You can create a pattern for bit-map and vector fills rather than using the file of CorelDRAW patterns.

Steps

1. Select the object you want to to use as the pattern.

2. Select Create Pattern from the Special menu. The Create Pattern dialog box appears.

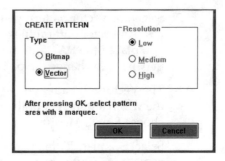

3. Select Bitmap or Vector. If you are creating a bit-map pattern, you also must select the Resolution.

4. Click OK. The cursor changes to crosshairs.

5. Press and hold down the mouse button and drag a marquee around the image you want to use as a pattern. Select only the tile image, even if it is only a portion of an object.

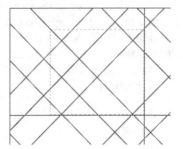

6. You are then be prompted for a file name.

7. Click Save, and the pattern is saved.

Notes

Bit-map patterns are added automatically to the library, but vector patterns must be named.

Even though you can capture any pattern in a CorelDRAW file, it is best to keep the pattern simple. CorelDRAW converts color bit maps to black and white. Diagonal lines in bit-map patterns can look jagged. Each vector tile is a miniature CorelDRAW file. If the tile has many objects or graduated fills, the patterned object may take a long time to print.

When you marquee-select a vector pattern, CorelDRAW picks up all the objects it needs to make that pattern, even if some of the elements extend beyond the marquee. You can reduce the complexity of the pattern by making sure that the pattern you want is not grouped or combined with any objects outside the tile.

Creating Linear and Radial Fountain Fills

Purpose

You can fill an object with two shades of a tint or color. Linear fountains change color in a straight line; radial fountains change colors in concentric circles.

Steps

1. Select the Fountain Fill icon. The Fountain Fill dialog box appears.

2. Select Linear or Radial.

3. If you select Linear, you must specify a fountain direction, or angle, in degrees. If you rotate the object, the fountain angle changes to keep the angle relative to the object.

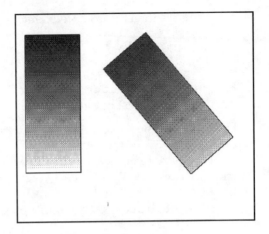

4. Select **S**pot or **P**rocess color.

5. Use the color palettes to select the beginning and ending colors. You can specify tints of **S**pot colors.

6. To increase the amount of start color in the fountain, click on the Optio**ns** button. The Fountain Fill Options dialog box appears.

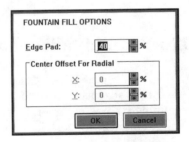

7. Add an **E**dge Pad setting. CorelDRAW fills an object's highlighting box, which can extend beyond the object for irregularly shaped or rotated objects. You can add some edge padding to compensate for this "lost" fill. Maximum edge pad value is 45 percent.

8. If you selected **R**adial, you can shift the center of the fill away from the center of the object. The maximum offset is 100 percent in either direction. This figure illustrates an Offset setting of 20 percent in both the **X** and **Y** directions.

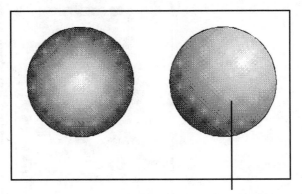

Radial offset of 20% X and 20% Y

9. If you selected **S**pot color, you may select from many PostScript settings. For special effects, like those shown, use a coarser screen in one of the many patterns provided:

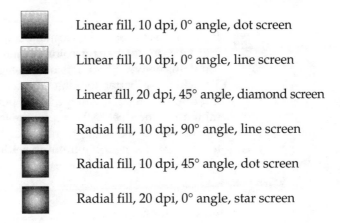

Linear fill, 10 dpi, 0° angle, dot screen

Linear fill, 10 dpi, 0° angle, line screen

Linear fill, 20 dpi, 45° angle, diamond screen

Radial fill, 10 dpi, 90° angle, line screen

Radial fill, 10 dpi, 45° angle, dot screen

Radial fill, 20 dpi, 0° angle, star screen

10. The last button on the flyout menu displays the PostScript Texture dialog box. These textures are miniature PostScript programs with several parameters that you can change.

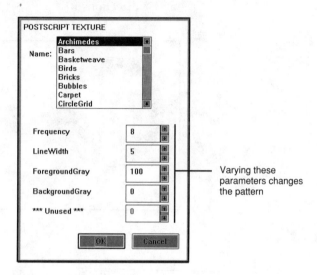

Varying these parameters changes the pattern

11. After you make all selections, click OK.

Notes

If you are using spot colors to make color separations and you do not have a color printer, only create fountains between two tints of the same spot color. To achieve a better looking fountain fill, set the minimum tint at greater than 0 percent. If the minimum tint is set to 0 percent, the fade gives out before the end of the object is reached. A value of five to 10 percent is a good minimum setting.

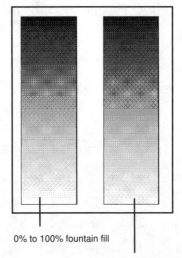

0% to 100% fountain fill

5% to 100% fountain fill

Note that PostScript textures are transparent and print in black only.

Consult Appendix A of the CorelDRAW documentation to see illustrations of all the PostScript texture files. You can generate millions of texture effects from these basic textures. Some textures are complex, and take a long time to print. The textures do not appear in the preview screen; instead a pattern of PS fills the object.

Using the Color Palette

Purpose

CorelDRAW lets you select from many colors on existing palettes and makes it easy to alter them into millions of others. You can arrange these colors on your palettes to suit your work.

Steps

1. Select the Outline tool. The Outline tool flyout menu appears.

2. Select the Custom Outline Color icon, the first icon in the second row. The Uniform Fill dialog box appears.

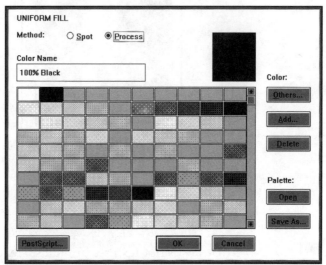

3. To select a color, click on the appropriate color swatch.

Notes

As a shortcut, select the object you want to fill, and then make a color selection from the palette bar that appears at the bottom on the screen.

Press Shift-F11 to display the Fill Color dialog box.

Press Shift-F12 to display the Outline Color dialog box.

CorelDRAW contains six color dialog boxes. Each dialog box pertains to a specific way to produce the colors you want: spot colors, named colors, CYMK, RGB, HSB, and process color.

Assigning Spot Color

Purpose

You can assign colors with the Pantone Matching System (PMS) and specify spot colors in percentages. If you print your drawing as a color separation, each spot color prints on a separate page.

Steps

1. Select the Uniform Fill or Outline Fill icon.

2. Select $\underline{S}$pot as the method of color.

3. Select the color you want to use from the palette.

4. You can search for a color by name if you select the $\underline{O}$thers option.

5. Click OK.

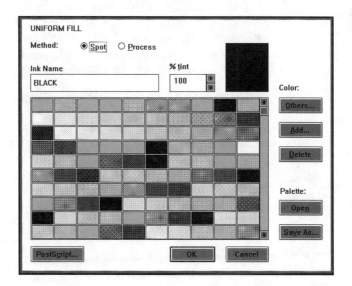

Notes

The spot colors you see on-screen often bear only a vague resemblance to actual PMS colors. PMS swatch books are available in most art supply stores. These swatches show you the actual PMS color.

You can use spot colors to break a drawing into layers. Just color all objects for a given layer with the same spot color. Then use the Print as Separations option to select the color layer you want to print. See also "Printing Color Separations."

One way to avoid using the Color menu frequently is to use the Copy **S**tyle From command to copy colors from existing objects. By creating a palette of temporary objects, you can add fill and outline colors to multiple objects.

You can rearrange the palette by dragging colors to a new location. Just click on the color and drag it to the desired position. To save your customized configuration (Version 2.01), see the discussion later in this chapter.

Double-clicking on a process color swatch displays the **O**thers color palette. Select **N**amed Colors, and change the selected color on the list. After you click OK, the new color is moved to that position on the palette. The old color moves over one square. Use this shortcut to assemble a custom palette.

To add spot color tints to the palette, double-click on one of the empty palette squares. After the Ink Colors dialog box appears, select a color and enter the desired tint. Click OK. If you are adding a tint in Version 2.01, click on the color for which you want to create a tint. Then click the **A**dd button. Enter the desired tint value in the Uniform Fill dialog box and click OK. The spot color tint is added to the palette beside the original color.

You can jump to the desired spot color by typing its name or number in the Search box. You do not need to type the word "Pantone."

Assigning Process Color

Purpose

This task enables you to combine four colors (cyan, magenta, yellow, and black) to create a custom or *process* color. Each color in the palette is a mixture of various percentages of these four process colors.

Steps

1. Select the Uniform Fill or Outline Fill icon.

2. Select <u>P</u>rocess as the method of color.

3. Select the color you want to use from the palette.

4. To create a custom color, select the <u>O</u>thers button. The Uniform Fill dialog box appears that enables you to create your own process color mix, based on three color models, CYMK, RGB, HSB and a named color option.

5. If you choose <u>C</u>MYK, specify the percentages for each of the four process colors. You can use the slider controls, or type the percentage you want to use in the box.

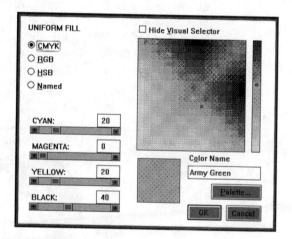

6. If you choose <u>R</u>GB, you specify percentages of red, green, and blue to mix colors. The advantage of this model is that it reproduces color much in the same way as your monitor does. The large square box controls the amount of red and green; the narrow box controls the amount of blue.

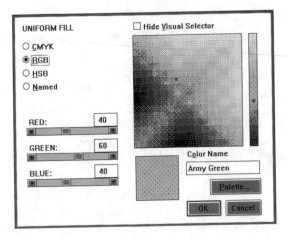

7. If you choose <u>H</u>SB, you work with three color parameters: Hue, Saturation, and Brightness. You use a color wheel to control the hue and saturation. The narrow box enables you to control brightness. Hue is specified by degrees by the position on the circle. Saturation and brightness are expressed in percentages.

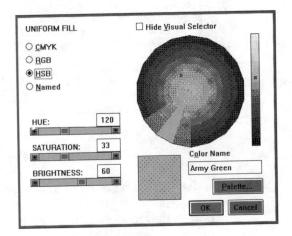

8. If you choose Named, you can select a color from a list. Note that you cannot edit the color names.

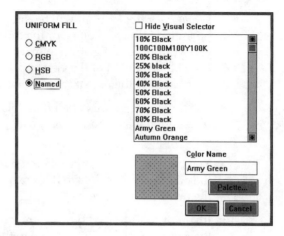

9. Click OK.

Notes

As you name colors, include the formula you used to obtain the color for future reference. An example is Tan_20C50M50Y20K.

When you print a drawing as color separations, one page prints for each process color used.

Predicting the actual printed color of a process color mix can be tricky. The final output depends on the printing press, the pressman, and other variables. Confer with your printer if you must have a precise color match.

Consider the following suggestions when using color:

- When your final output will be different sheets separated into spot colors, or the four process colors, give your printer registration marks for alignment. Use character 0184 of the Geographic font (circle with crosshairs) as the registration mark.

- Use a 100-percent mix of all four colors to produce registration marks and labels on all pages of the color separations.

- You can get a blacker black if you add a percentage of the other process colors to it. Consult your printer for the preferred mixture.

- If you print text-sized type in a mix of process colors, the text may appear ragged due to the screens that make up the tint. Try to have at least one solid color other than yellow in your mix for text.

- For projects that require a consistent color palette, such as slide presentations, create a custom palette of only those colors.

- Give your custom palette the same name as the CorelDRAW file it is used with. CorelDRAW saves the palette with the PAL extension. This process makes it easy for you to copy, move, and delete the file and its associated palette.

- Note that in Version 2.0, you can delete colors only by editing the CORELDRW.PAL file with a text editor such as Windows Notepad. In Version 2.01, however, use the Delete button in the Color dialog box. If you make unwanted color deletions, you can re-store the original process color palette by loading CorelDRAW's backup palette, PURE99.PAL. You should make a backup of the spot color palette as well. Save a copy under the name SPOTBACK.PAL.

Converting Spot Color to Process Color

Purpose

CorelDRAW can convert any spot color to its process color equivalent.

Steps

1. Select the spot color you want to convert.
2. Select <u>P</u>rocess as the method of color.
3. Select the <u>O</u>thers option.
4. Select <u>C</u>MYK as the color model.
5. Type a name for the color and click OK. The color is saved to the process color palette.

Notes

Not all spot colors have precise CMYK equivalents. You can gauge the result by referring to Pantone's Spot Color equivalent books.

If you do not specify a color name, the color is applied as unnamed color.

Setting the Default Fill and Outline Settings

Purpose

You can control the default Fill and Outline settings, including color, that CorelDRAW uses when an object is created.

Steps

1. Make sure that no object is selected by clicking on a blank area.
2. Select any of the Outline or Fill flyout menu boxes. The New Object Uniform Fill dialog box appears.

3. You can apply the new object settings to **A**ll Objects, **T**ext Objects, or **O**ther Objects.

4. Click OK and the appropriate fill or outline dialog box appears.

Notes

You can change the default palette from **P**rocess to **S**pot color by changing the new object setting for object fill. Note that gray screens in both the Outline and Fill flyout menus are process colors, regardless of which palette is active.

Set the fill to Black and the outline to None for text. Text displays faster without an outline. For other objects, set the Fill to None and the Outline to .5 point or so. These settings enable you to see everything in the Preview.

If you plan to create many objects with nondefault settings, spend a few minutes setting up the desired defaults before you begin the drawing. This technique saves you the trouble of changing objects later on.

Copying Outline and Fill Styles

Purpose

You can copy the outline and fill styles from one object to another object.

Steps

1. Select the object that you want to change.

2. From the Edit menu, select Copy Style From. The Copy Style dialog box appears.

3. Choose the parameters you want to copy and click OK.

4. Click on the object you want to copy from using the From? arrow.

Notes

Press Ctrl-R to repeat the Copy Style From command.

Create temporary objects with any complex outlines and fills and then use the Copy Style From command to apply them to objects.

Trapping Colors

Purpose

Trapping is a technique used in printing to ensure that two adjacent colors overlap slightly so that no unprinted white area shows up in the printed job.

Although CorelDRAW has no automatic trapping function, you can use several methods to create a trap. In all cases, apply the trap as a last step in your drawing.

Steps

To trap filled objects, follow these steps:

1. Select the lighter object.

2. Give it an outline of .3 points in the same color as the object. A trap of .15 points is created because the outline is centered on the object.

3. Choose Overprint in the PostScript Controls dialog box for the outline.

To trap a line, follow these steps:

1. Create a duplicate of the object on the top of the original (Ctrl-D).

2. Increase the stroke of the duplicate by .3 points and designate it to overprint.

3. Make sure the line caps overlap the endpoints on both objects.

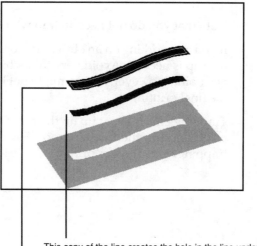

This copy of the line creates the hole in the line underneath

This thicker copy of the line creates the trap

To trap outline objects, follow these steps:

1. If the object has an outline of a different color than the object, duplicate the object (Ctrl-D).

2. Increase the stroke of the duplicate by .3 points.

3. Set the object to overprint.

4. Set the fill of the duplicate to None.

Create copy of object with thicker outline and no fill

Notes

Note that you do not need to trap white objects.

If you are working on an object that contains a white outline, no trap is needed. Avoid very thin white outlines (less than one point), however, as they might not look evenly spaced in the final printing.

Trapping effects show up on the proof you receive from the printer and in the final artwork. For more information on trapping, consult your printer.

CHAPTER 8

Special Effects

This chapter shows you how to use the commands from the Effects menu. CorelDRAW's powerful effects enable you to change the shape and color of objects and to type with ease.

You learn to shape two-dimensional objects with the Envelope functions and **B**lend command. You also learn to add dimension to any object and to add dimension to any object or type by using the E**x**trude and **P**erspective effects.

This chapter discusses the following operations and concepts:

- Extruding objects to add dimensional effects to your drawing

- Blending objects from one shape to another

- Using Envelope to stretch and distort objects

- Changing the perspective of an extruded object

Introducing **E**xtrude

The **E**xtrude command gives an object a three-dimensional appearance. That is, it adds visual depth to the drawing. After an extrusion is performed, the results are placed as a series of grouped objects behind the original. There are two different types of extrusion: parallel and perspective. Each type of extrusion is discussed in the following sections.

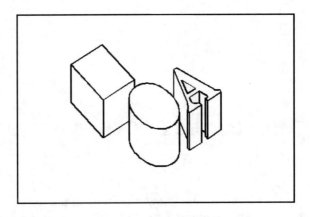

Notes

Only one object can be extruded at a time, and groups of objects or grouped objects cannot be extruded.

Creating a Parallel Extrusion

Purpose

The lines of the results from this type of extrusion are drawn parallel to each other.

Steps

1. Select the object to be extruded.

2. Select Extrude from the Effects menu. The Extrude dialog box appears.

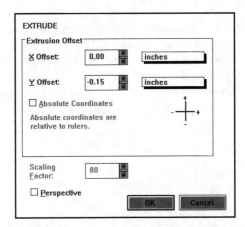

3. Set the **X** and **Y** Offsets to determine the distance and direction of the extrusion. See the figure in the following Notes section for more information on controlling the offset.

4. Be sure that the **P**erspective check box is not checked, then click OK. The extrusion appears as a set of grouped objects placed behind the original object, with the fill and outline attributes of the original.

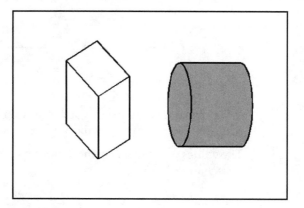

 Unfilled objects are extruded with all line segments visible, creating a "wireframe" effect. Filled objects only extrude the visible sides.

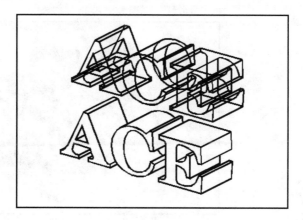

Notes

Control the direction of the extrusion by setting the values for X and Y to positive and negative values.

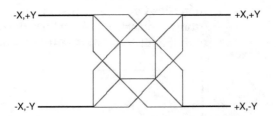

If the object is complex, or your computer is relatively slow, this process may take a while.

The values you have set in the dialog box remain in effect until you change them.

 You can enhance the extrusion effect by coloring the various extruded shapes with different fills. Ungroup the extrusion, fill the shapes, then regroup the objects to keep everything aligned. (See Chapter 7 for more information on fills.)

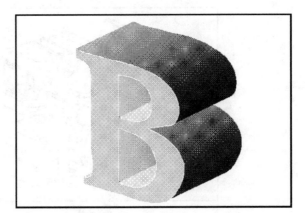

Creating a Perspective Extrusion

Purpose

In a perspective extrusion, the resulting object projects toward a vanishing point.

Steps

1. Select the object to be extruded.

2. Select Extrude from the Effects menu.

3. Set the **X** and **Y** Offsets to shift the vanishing point away from the center of the object. See the figure from the preceding Notes section for more information on controlling the offset.

4. Select **P**erspective in the dialog box.

5. Select a Scaling **F**actor. A scale of less than 100% puts the vanishing point behind the object. A scaling factor of 0 extrudes the sides all the way to the vanishing point; a scale of more than 100% pulls the vanishing point in front of the object.

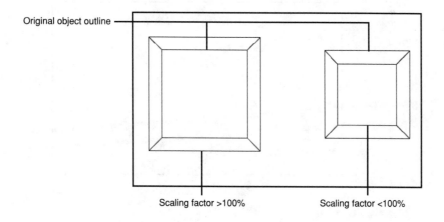

Original object outline

Scaling factor >100%   Scaling factor <100%

6. Click OK.

If you use **P**erspective on a filled object with the scaling factor below 100, be sure that the vanishing point is outside the object. Otherwise, the extrusion is hidden by the object. To correct this problem, unfill the object or relocate the vanishing point outside the object.

Using **A**bsolute Coordinates

The **A**bsolute Coordinates option enables you to specify an exact numerical location on the drawing for the vanishing point. This option enables you to draw many objects with the same vanishing point, just as they do in reality.

To extrude to an exact point, move the rulers to the desired point, then set the X and Y coordinates to 0. (See Chapter 1 for more information on moving rulers.)

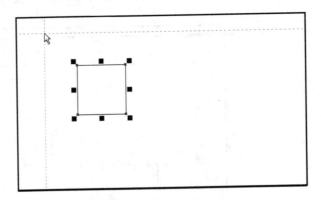

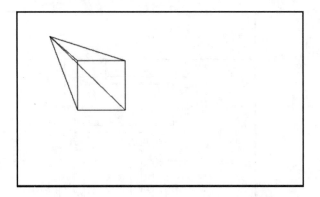

Creating Uniform Beveled Edges

Purpose

Perspective Extrusion is handy for making beveled edges, but if the shape is anything other than a square, the short sides are fatter than the long sides. The following steps show you how to create uniform edges.

Steps

1. Create a square and perspective extrude it to the bevel thickness desired. Leave X and Y coordinates at 0. Use the scaling factor to adjust bevel width.

2. Ungroup the extruded objects.

3. Combine all the ungrouped objects with the original square.

4. Change to the shape tool.

5. Drag nodes to create the desired rectangle.

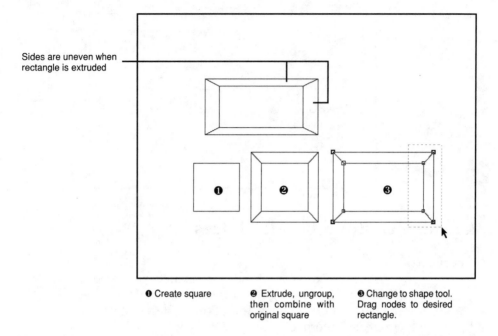

Sides are uneven when
rectangle is extruded

❶ Create square

❷ Extrude, ungroup,
then combine with
original square

❸ Change to shape tool.
Drag nodes to desired
rectangle.

6. Return to the Pick tool to break the objects apart and fill as desired.

7. Regroup the objects to retain the proper alignment.

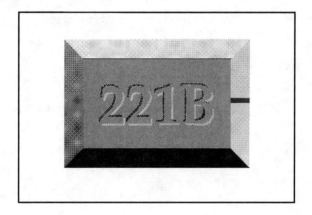

CorelDRAW creates the extruded shapes based on the nodes on the object. Thus if you add points to a path, more extruded shapes are created.

Blending Objects

Purpose

The **B**lend command creates the appearance of an object progressively changing its shape, such as from a square to a circle.

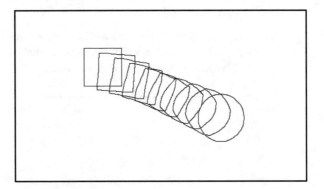

Steps

1. Create and select the two objects to be blended.

2. Select **B**lend from the Effe**c**ts menu. The **B**lend dialog box appears.

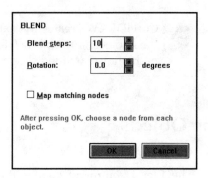

3. Enter the number of steps desired. The maximum number is 200. Use as few steps as necessary to create the desired effect.

4. To rotate the shapes as they blend, select a **R**otation value. Positive values rotate clockwise; negative values rotate counterclockwise.

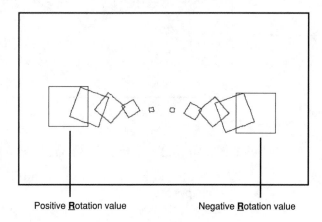

Positive **R**otation value   Negative **R**otation value

If you move the center of rotation for the two objects before blending, the intermediate shapes form an arc.

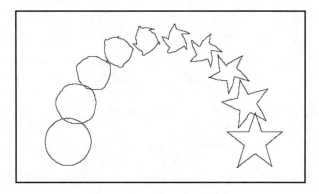

5. Click OK. The objects are blended.

Notes

The keyboard shortcut for **B**lend is Ctrl-B.

Using the **M**ap Matching Nodes Command

Purpose

Objects are blended based on the locations of the beginning nodes of each object. By selecting **M**ap Matching Nodes you can specify the beginning nodes for each object.

Steps

1. Select **M**ap Matching Nodes and click OK. The cursor changes to a bent arrow, and the nodes on one object appear.

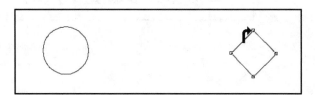

2. Select the desired starting node, and click. The arrow flips over, and the second object is highlighted.

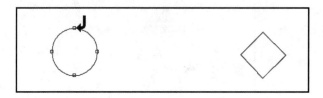

3. Select the starting node for the second object.

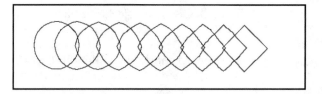

 If the objects being blended have a different number of paths, the intermediate objects contain open paths.

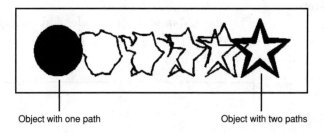

Object with one path   Object with two paths

Use **B**lend to create a palette of tints for a spot or process color. For spot colors, create a square with the desired color. Duplicate the square, and set the tint of the duplicate to 0%. Spread them apart far enough that the intermediates do not overlap. Then blend. Nine steps give you 10% increments of the color. Then use Copy **S**tyle From to copy the desired tints as needed.

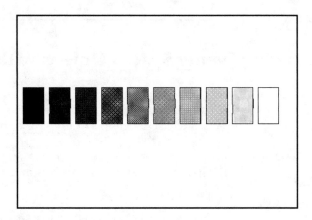

Creating Concentric Circles or Squares with **B**lend

Purpose

Blend provides a quick and convenient way to create a series of evenly spaced concentric circles or squares.

Steps

1. Create and duplicate a circle or square.

2. Shrink or enlarge the duplicate. Hold the Shift key down to keep the two objects centered.

3. Blend the two objects.

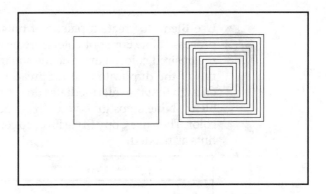

Drawing Evenly Spaced Objects with Blend

Purpose

You can also use **B**lend to create series of evenly spaced objects, such as tick marks or lines for a chart.

Steps

1. Create the first and last objects and select them.

2. Blend the two objects.

Note that when rectangles, ellipses, and text are blended, the intermediate objects are converted to curves.

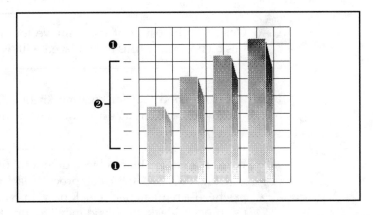

❶ Draw these marks...   ❷ ...Then blend to make these marks

Creating Highlighting and Airbrush Effects

Use **B**lend to create irregularly-shaped fountain fills. Illustrators use this technique to create highlights on objects. Blends created this way display and print a bit faster than fountain fills. But be careful: it is easy to create hundreds of objects this way, resulting in huge files that may not print.

Objects with postscript, fountain, vector or bitmap fills blend, but the fills are replaced with white.

Blend is also a good tool for creating "neon" effects with objects and type. See Chapter 4 for more information on type.

 When blending a black object, do not fill the object with the 100C100Y100M100K process black from the palette; use regular black (100K only) instead. If you use process black, the blend may "fill up" too soon and print in uneven colors.

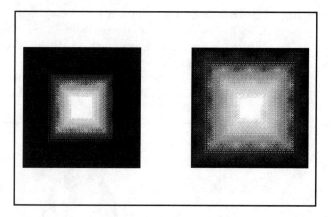

 If you blend two objects that have different spot colors, the intermediate objects have process colors.

Editing an Object Envelope

Purpose

The Envelope functions enable you to distort an object, stretching it as if it were made of rubber.

Steps

1. Select the object or group with the Pick tool.

2. Click on Edit Envelope from the Effects menu. A flyout menu appears.

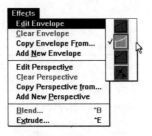

3. Select one of the four edit modes from the flyout menu:

- **Straight Line.** The segments of the envelope behave as straight lines.

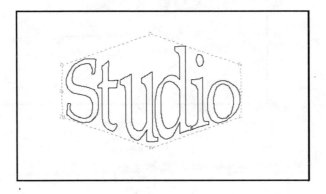

- **Single Arc.** The sides of the envelope behave as smooth curves. This mode gives the object a "squeezed" appearance.

- **Compound Arc.** Top and bottom curves can change direction, creating S-curves. You can use this effect to make the text look like it is going over a hill, for example.

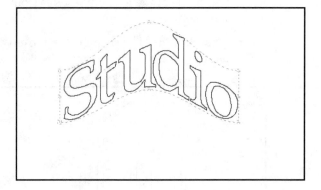

- **Nonconstrained.** All nodes can move independently. Unlike the other modes, you can select more than one node at a time for editing.

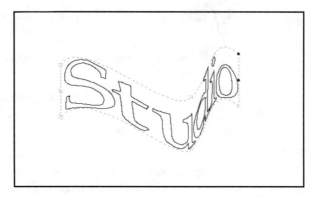

A highlighting box with handles (an envelope) appears around the object.

4. Move the handles with the cursor to distort the envelope.

 Use E<u>d</u>it Envelope to create curved shapes, It can be faster than manipulating individual nodes of an object, especially when a symmetrical effect is needed. Experiment with the various Envelope modes to get a feel for their effect on different shapes.

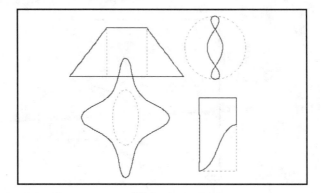

Notes

Text distorted with E_d_it Envelope can still be edited.

The following key combinations constrain the envelope edit:

- **Ctrl-drag**. Moves the oppposite node in the same direction
- **Shift-drag**. Moves the opposite node in the opposite direction
- **Ctrl-Shift-drag**. Moves all four sides at once.

Other Envelope Operations

- **Copy Envelope F_r_om.** Like Copy _S_tyle From, this command enables you to copy an envelope effect from one object to another.

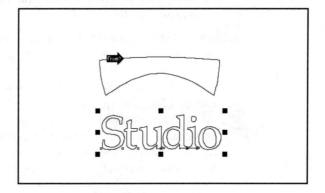

- **Add New Envelope**. After you have distorted an object using Envelope, you can add another envelope to the object by selecting Add New Envelope. The highlight box changes back to a rectangle.

 Use Add New Envelope to use more than one envelope editing mode on an object.

- **Clear Envelope**. This option deletes the envelope and restores the object to its original shape. If more than one envelope has been applied to the object, then only the most recent envelope is removed. To remove all envelopes at once, use Clear Transformations.

Editing Perspective

Purpose

This feature enables you to apply a true one- or two-point perspective to an object or group of objects. The effect of Edit Perspective is different from Edit Envelope, in that the more distant parts of the object are drawn smaller, as they would appear in three dimensions.

Steps

1. Select an object (or group of objects) with the Pick tool.

2. Select Edit Perspective from the Effects menu. A highlighting box with four corner handles appears around the object.

3. Move the handles to distort the object.

Notes

After an object has a perspective applied to it, selecting the Node Edit tool activates the Perspective Edit mode.

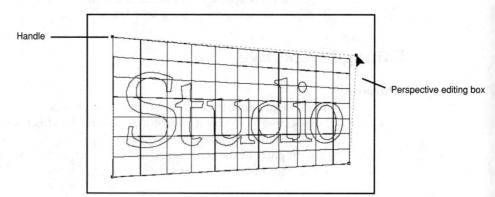

The following key combinations constrain the perspective edit:

- **Ctrl-drag.** Constrains movement to horizontal or vertical directions

- **Ctrl-Shift-drag.** Moves opposite nodes in the opposite direction.

Other Perspective Operations

- **Two-Point Perspective**. Move one or more handles diagonally to create a two-point perspective effect.

- **Vanishing Points**. If you move two handles close enough together, one or both vanishing points appear on screen. You can drag these points to alter the perspective.

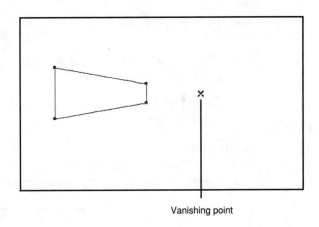

Vanishing point

 If you move the vanishing points too close to the object, the perspective distortion is undone.

- **Add New Perspective**. Select Add New Perspective to layer perspectives on an object. The perspective box changes back to a rectangle.

- **Clear Perspective**. Clears the distortion of the object. If there are multiple perspectives on an object, Clear Perspective only clears the most recently applied perspective. Clear Transformations removes all perspectives at once.

- **Copy Perspective from**. Copies the perspective distortion from one object to another. Highlight the object to copy to, click Copy Perspective from, and select the object to copy from.

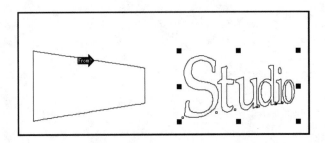

To speed your work when distorting complex paths, such as text strings, distort a rectangle of the same dimensions, then use Copy Perspective.

 Use guidelines to align vanishing points precisely. This is useful if you are working with multiple objects with the same perspective. (See Chapter 1 for more information on creating guidelines.)

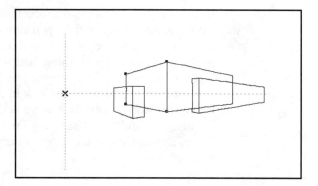

 Use Perspective to make alignment grids to use when creating 3-dimensional illustrations. Group the grids together and send to back, so they are out of the way when you draw or edit nodes.

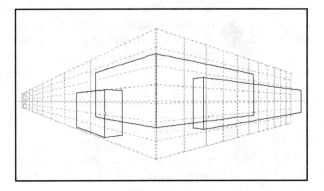

 If you apply an envelope to an object, and then apply a perspective on top of that, you cannot remove the underlying envelope without removing the perspective. (The same thing happens when you layer an envelope over a perspective. To remove the "bottom" effect, make a duplicate of the object. Use Clear Transformations to remove both effects from the original, and then use Copy Envelope or Copy Perspective to copy the "top" effect back to the original object.)

❶ Perspective added to object
❷ Envelope added atop perspective
❸ Copy both effects to second object
❹ Use Clear Transformations on original object
❺ Copy Envelope from second object

To apply Perspective or Envelope to more than one object at a time, the objects must first be grouped. You can ungroup the objects after applying the effect.

When you use convert to curves an object that has envelope or perspective applied, the objects keep their shape; however, all paths are converted to curves. All Envelopes and Perspectives are removed at once. Each effect applied to an object roughly doubles the number of points that are created when the object is converted to curves. This can lead to "bumpy" paths, especially on text objects.

CHAPTER 9

Printing

This chapter discusses the printing options available in the CorelDRAW Print dialog box and provides helpful information for preparing your file for output to an imagesetter or by a service bureau. Note that some of the options discussed apply only to PostScript printers as indicated. In this chapter, you also learn to use the Print Merge command to insert variable text strings into files you use repeatedly, such as name tags and certificates.

Using the Print Command

Purpose

You often want to print the file after completing a drawing. The following section discusses the many options and settings available in the Print dialog box.

Steps

1. To print a file, select Print from the File menu. The Print Options dialog box appears.

```
PRINT OPTIONS [POSTSCRIPT]

□ Print Only Selected          Number Of Copies:        1
□ Fit To Page                  □ Scale:                 100      %
□ Tile
□ Print As Separations         Fountain Stripes:        128
□ Crop Marks & Crosshairs      Flatness:                1.00
□ Film Negative
                               ┌Default Screen Frequency
□ Include File Info            ● Device's
    □ Within Page              ○ Custom:         60       Per Inch
□ All Fonts Resident

┌Destination                   □ Print to File          □ For Mac
 PostScript Printer
 LPT1:                         [ Printer Setup... ]  [ OK ]  [ Cancel ]
```

2. Select the print options you want to use, then click on OK.

   You can select the following options from the Print Options dialog box:

- Print Only Selected enables you to print only the currently highlighted objects.

- Fit To Page enables you to scale a graphic to fit the current page size. The entire graphic is scaled. If it is smaller than the page size, the graphic is enlarged to fill the page. If it is larger than the page size, the graphic is scaled down to fit on the page.

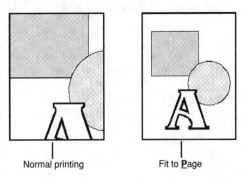

Normal printing   Fit to Page

Fit To Page scales the graphic, but you have no record of the reduction percentage. If you need to know the reduction percentage, use Scale.

- **T**ile enables you to print a file in sections (tiles) if the file is too big to fit on the current page size. The tiles overlap slightly so you can piece the entire image together. You cannot modify the amount of overlap.

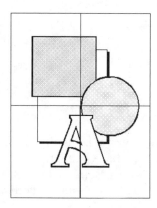

- Print As S**e**parations (PostScript printers only) enables you to print a file as color separations. If you use process colors in the file, a page is printed for each of the four process colors. If you use spot colors, a page is printed for each spot color. If you combine spot and process colors, a page is printed for each different color.

  When you select Print as S**e**parations, CorelDRAW automatically turns on Crop Ma**r**ks & Crosshairs, Film **N**egative, and Include File **I**nfo. You may deselect these options if you do not want them to print.

When you deselect Print As S**e**parations, the Crop Ma**r**ks & Crosshairs, Film **N**egative, and Include File **I**nfo options remain selected. You must deselect them manually.

After you click on OK, the Color Separations dialog box appears.

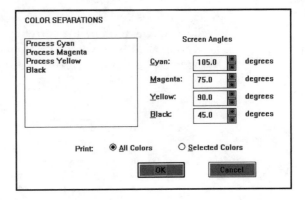

You can print all the colors or only selected colors in
the file. CorelDRAW sets the default screen angles to
avoid *Moiré distortions*, or "flickering" optical
patterns. Usually, you do not have to modify these
settings.

The screen frequency is set with the Default Screen
Frequency option (discussed later in this section).
Any special screens set for individual objects with
the PostScript options for Fill or Outline (see Chapter 7) override the default setting.

If you set nondefault screens for an object with a spot
color fill and later convert the color to process, those
settings are lost.

- Crop Mar**k**s & Crosshairs (PostScript only) enables
  you to print *crop marks*, which show the page boun-
  daries, and *registration marks* (crosshairs), which help
  the pressman align the separations when printing.
  You must print to a sheet size that is larger than the
  page size of your file, or shrink the page size, for crop
  marks and crosshairs to show. This setting is selected
  automatically when you select Print As S**e**parations.

- Film **N**egative (PostScript only) enables you to print a file as a negative (with the image reversed). When you print to film with an imagesetter, the image is created with the emulsion down. This setting also is selected automatically when you select Print As Separations.

Be sure to tell your service bureau that your CorelDRAW file is set to print as a negative. Otherwise, when you request negatives, the service bureau sets its equipment to also print a negative image. This setup gives you a negative of a negative, which results as a film positive.

- Include File **I**nfo (PostScript only) enables you to print the file name, current date and time, color name, and screen angle outside the left margin of the page. To make this information appear on the printed page, print to a larger sheet or select the **W**ithin Page option. **W**ithin Page enables you to print the file information inside the left margin of the page. The position is fixed, and the file information is printed over any objects in the same position.

- All Fonts **R**esident (PostScript only) enables CorelDRAW to treat all fonts as resident in the printer. Use All Fonts **R**esident if all the fonts used in your file have been downloaded to your printer. The files print faster. Use this option when sending files to a service bureau only if the bureau has all the fonts you are using. (The bureau's fonts must be *exactly* the same fonts.) In general, do not select this option when sending files to a service bureau so you do not have to worry about whether the bureau has the necessary fonts.

Any font not resident in the output device is printed in Courier. In addition, letter spacing may vary slightly between the CorelDRAW version and the resident version of a font if they are not exactly the same.

- Number Of Copies enables you to control the number of copies to print. This setting overrides the Windows Control Panel setting for the number of copies.

- Scale enables you to scale the printed output up or down. The scaling origin is the upper left corner for non-PostScript printers and the bottom left corner for PostScript printers.

Large objects with fountain fills show banding on laser printers, especially at higher screen resolutions. To evaluate a design, print it at 50 percent or smaller. The fountains appear smoother.

- Fountain Stripes (PostScript only) enables you to control the number of stripes used to create a fountain fill. The more stripes you use, the smoother the fill appears; however, the file takes longer to print. For imagesetters, use 128 stripes (the default setting) for a 1,270 dots per inch (dpi) resolution and 200 stripes for a 2,540 dpi resolution. Fountain stripes for non-PostScript printers are set under the Preferences menu (see Chapter 1).

With most PostScript laser printers, as you increase the screen frequency, the number of fountain stripes decreases. If you want a smooth fountain, print the file at a larger size and lower screen frequency, then reduce it on a photocopier.

- Flatness (PostScript only) enables you to control the smoothness of curves. PostScript uses short, straight segments to make up curves. For these curves to appear smooth, many segments must be created. Use the Flatness setting to determine the length of these segments.

 Objects with a large number of segments may not print. Increasing the Flatness setting often overcomes this problem. Imagesetters are more prone to this problem than laser printers because imagesetters' high-resolution output requires several times more line segments. An image that prints on a laser printer may not print on an imagesetter. To test printability, you can simulate printing a file on an imagesetter by decreasing the Flatness setting to .25.

If a file does not print on an imagesetter, try increasing the Flatness setting to 2 or 4.

- Default Screen Frequency (PostScript only) enables you to set the screen frequency for all objects except those that have special Outline and Fill settings applied with the PostScript option (see Chapter 7). The Device's setting enables you to print a file at the default frequency of the printer—usually 60 lines-per-inch for laser printers and 120 or 150 lines-per-inch for imagesetters. Custom enables you to select a frequency other than the device's default.

 Your output tends to darken when printed at higher line frequencies. Print a test file if you need a precise screen density. With laser printers, any resolution higher than 90 lines-per-inch darken considerably.

- Print to **F**ile enables you to send the print output to a file. Use this option to send a file to a service bureau for imagesetter output. The program assigns the file the extension PRN.

Printing to a floppy disk is time-consuming, especially for large files. You can save time by printing to a directory on your hard disk, or to a RAM disk if you have one, and then moving the files with DOS or Windows File Manager after you finish working with CorelDRAW.

- For **M**ac enables you to remove from the print file the Ctrl-D characters that can prevent files from printing on Mac-driven systems. Check with your service bureau for the best way to send CorelDRAW files. Some service bureaus prefer to print EPS files exported from CorelDRAW rather than from the CorelDRAW file itself.

In some versions of the Windows Print Driver, a bug exists that may prevent 11-by-17-inch size images from printing properly. Print Driver Version 3.4 is especially troublesome. Check with your service bureau before sending large-size output. If you have problems, call CorelDRAW's technical support department for more information.

- Destination shows the currently selected printer. You can change printers by using the Windows Control Panel.

- Printer **S**etup enables you to access the Windows Printer Setup dialog box, from which you can select the printer type and other options.

Use the CorelDRAW Print Options dialog box to set the output resolution and number of copies. These settings override the Windows Printer Setup settings.

 Windows and CorelDRAW do not always update the page orientation automatically when you switch between landscape and portrait files. Check the page orientation before printing, especially if you have just opened a file.

 Drawing files may take a long time to print if they contain any of the following items:

- Fountain fills

- PostScript textures

- Bit maps

- Bit-map fills

- Vector fills

- Large amounts of type

- Objects with large numbers of points (more than 500)

- Files with large numbers of objects

 If a file does not print, try breaking it into smaller segments or printing only selected objects. If you encounter frequent problems, you may need to add more memory to your printer.

With non-PostScript laser printers, reducing the resolution from 300 dpi to 75 dpi through the Control Panel greatly speeds up printing. This method is useful for proofing your work prior to final printing.

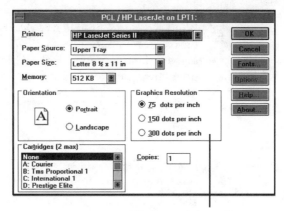

Reduce resolution setting
to speed printing

 Printing to the Print Manager frees up your computer more quickly, but it slows down printing time. See the section on using the Print Manager in your *Windows User Guide*.

Notes

The keyboard shortcut for Print is Ctrl-P.

Using the Print Merge Command

Purpose

Replaces the text strings in a CorelDRAW file with other text strings from a merge file. This command is useful for making certificates, name tags, business cards, or anything with a standard layout and variable text.

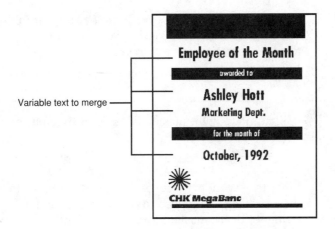

Variable text to merge

Steps

1. Set up the master drawing exactly as you want it to appear. The merged text takes on all the attributes of the text in the master drawing; however, individual changes within a string may not always be applied to the merged text. Use generic text references, such as "name" and "date."

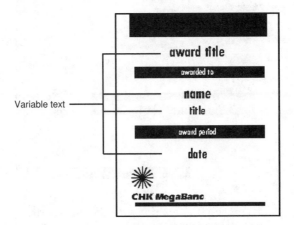

Variable text

2. Create a merge text file by using a word processor that enables you to save the text as an ASCII text file, with a TXT extension. On the first line of the file, indicate the number of variable text strings. Then

enter the master strings exactly as they appear in the CorelDRAW file, with backslashes (\) before and after the text. You can put each string on a separate line for readability.

 Use numbers in the master file to lessen the chance of typing mistakes.

3. Enter the secondary strings to be substituted for the master strings. You need to type a corresponding string for every master string. If you want a line to be blank, type spaces. You must surround secondary strings with backslashes, also. Enter as many sets of secondary strings as you want. Save the completed file in ASCII format.

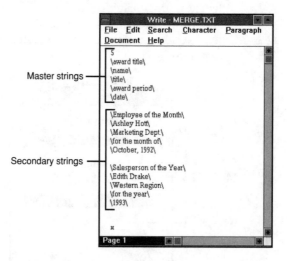

4. To merge the text file with the master drawing, open the master drawing and select Print **M**erge from the **F**ile menu.

5. Select the text file and click on Merge.

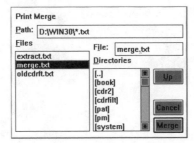

The Print Options box appears, as in normal printing.

6. Click on OK to print.

CHAPTER 10

Managing Files

CorelDRAW and Windows work together to help you organize, view, and save your files. This chapter teaches you various techniques for quickly locating drawings you have saved. It also discusses importing files from other applications and exporting your CorelDRAW files for use in other programs. You also learn to use AutoTrace and the CorelTRACE utility to prepare imported files for editing.

This chapter discusses the following tasks and procedures:

- Using MOSAIC
- Locating and opening directories and files
- Using the MOSAIC library
- Using SlideShow
- Importing and exporting files
- Using AutoTrace
- Using CorelTRACE
- Customizing tracing options
- Tracing manually

Activating MOSAIC

Purpose

CorelDRAW's MOSAIC utility is a "visual file manager" that enables you to access, archive, and manipulate CorelDRAW files.

Steps

You can access MOSAIC from within CorelDRAW or from the Windows Program Manager.

To open MOSAIC from Windows:

1. Open the Windows Program Manager.

2. Double-click on the MOSAIC icon in the CorelDRAW Applications Group, which was automatically created when you installed CorelDRAW.

To open MOSAIC from CorelDRAW:

1. From the **S**pecial menu, select Pr**e**ferences.

2. Click the **U**se MOSAIC box.

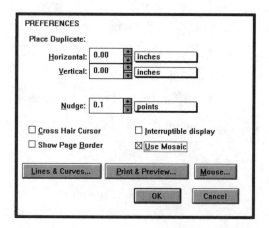

Now when you choose **O**pen or **I**mport (CDR files only) from the **F**ile menu, MOSAIC is activated.

In either mode:

3. From the File menu, choose Select Directory, or press Ctrl-S.

```
File  Library  Special
Select Directory...  ^S
Open                 ^O
Delete              Del
Get Info...          ^G
Import               ^I
Export...            ^E
Print...             ^P
Select by Keyword... ^K
Select All           ^A
Exit                 ^X
```

4. Select a directory and click OK to return to the visual display.

5. Select files in the visual display by moving the highlighting box with the mouse or arrow keys. The scroll bar enables you to display additional files in the directory. Selected files reverse color.

   Press End once to move the highlight box to the end of the row. Press End a second time to move to the bottom right of the screen, and press End a third time to move to the last file in the directory. Press Home to move toward the beginning of the list.

6. Double-click on a file icon to load that file into CorelDRAW. (If you are in the *standalone mode*, or working directly from Windows, CorelDRAW opens, then the file loads.) Although MOSAIC is minimized, it remains active.

7. To exit MOSAIC, choose Exit from the File menu or press Ctrl-X. If you are in standalone mode, you return to Windows. In CorelDRAW mode, you return to CorelDRAW.

Notes

If you are in CorelDRAW, all CDR files in the current directory are displayed. MOSAIC uses the image header discussed in Chapter 1 to display the files.

CorelDRAW 1.x files lack image headers and appear as boxes with a line through them. To add an image header to these files, resave them as 2.0 files.

You can delete selected files in standalone mode by choosing **D**elete from the **F**ile menu.

The keyboard shortcuts in MOSAIC are inconsistent with those in CorelDRAW.

Getting Information about Files

You can get specific information about a file by choosing the **G**et Info option from the **F**ile menu or by pressing Ctrl-G. This option displays an information screen that contains the name of the file, the date (in Canadian format) you last modified the file, the file size, file attributes, and the image header.

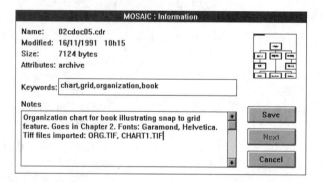

The MOSAIC Information dialog box also contains a field in which you can add information to a file listing. The *Keywords* field enables you to perform database searches for a specific word or words among groups of files in the current directory. Simply enter descriptive words separated with commas (logical *or*) or with pluses (logical *and*) in this field. The *Notes* field enables you to annotate your work. You can use this field to keep a record of nonstandard typefaces and file names of bit maps used in a CorelDRAW file, for example.

Using the MOSAIC Library

Purpose

MOSAIC uses a version of the LHARC file-compression utility to compress and store multiple CorelDRAW files in single files called *libraries*. Libraries consist of two types of files—CLB files and CLH files.

Steps

1. Open MOSAIC from the Windows Program Manager.

2. Select the Library menu.

3. Choose from the following options:

   • Select Library loads a library into MOSAIC. The contents of the library appear on the MOSAIC screen.

   • Expand Image(s) to CDR decompresses one or more files in the library and copies them to the directory you select. The compressed version remains in the library.

   • Delete Library deletes an entire library. Only the compressed files in the library are erased, not the original CorelDRAW files.

Notes

If you copy or move libraries, you must move both the .CLB and .CLH files.

 If you are decompressing files from libraries, make sure that you have enough disk space to store the files. Use the Expand option to determine the space required for the decompressed files and the space that you have available.

If a library contains the only copies of your CorelDRAW files, specify the library as a read-only file to prevent accidental deletion.

To use the clip art that comes with CorelDRAW, you must extract the art from the libraries in MOSAIC. To reduce access time, copy the files from the original floppy disks to a directory on your hard disk. Copy both the .CLB and .CLH files.

MOSAIC can be a memory hog and may slow your system considerably if it has a limited amount of memory. If this is the case, use MOSAIC in the standalone mode only.

Archiving is not foolproof. If you use Library to store CorelDRAW files and plan to delete the original files, be sure you can read the compressed files before you delete the original files.

If you are concerned about losing a CorelDRAW file, save the file in decompressed format on a floppy disk and store the disk in a safe place. The price of a floppy disk is nothing compared to the inconvenience of rebuilding a complex file from scratch.

To change from viewing a library to viewing CorelDRAW files, choose Select Directory from the File menu. Then select the directory that contains the CorelDRAW files you want to view. When MOSAIC is in Library mode, the name of the library file appears at the top of the MOSAIC screen. You can not add files to a library when MOSAIC is in Library mode.

Creating and Adding Images to a Library

Purpose

You can add CorelDRAW files to a library, or create a new library.

Steps

1. From the MOSAIC file display, highlight one or more images.

2. From the <u>L</u>ibrary menu, select <u>A</u>dd Image(s) to Library. The <u>A</u>dd Images to Library dialog box appears.

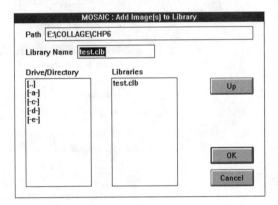

3. Select the library to which you want to add files, or create a new library by typing a name in the Library Name box.

4. Click OK. The selected CorelDRAW files are copied into the library in compressed format. The original CorelDRAW files remain intact.

Notes

You cannot move a file from one library to another. Only decompressed files can be added to a library.

To combine libraries, expand all the files from the separate libraries into a common directory, select all files, and create a new library to contain the files. Then delete the old libraries.

Using SlideShow

Purpose

SlideShow is a special utility that enables you to present selected CorelDRAW files at specified intervals. When used with special multimedia equipment, SlideShow helps you create and present an automated slide show directly from your computer.

Steps

1. Select two or more CorelDRAW files from the MOSAIC file display to use in your slide show.

2. From the Special menu, select SlideShow. The SlideShow dialog box appears.

3. Adjust the delay that you want to occur between slide presentations. Choose from the following options:

   • **Manual.** Enables you to control the advancement of slides by clicking the mouse.

   • **Automatic.** Runs unattended. You set the time delay (in seconds) that you want to occur between slide presentations.

   • **Continuous.** Displays slides until you press Esc.

Notes

The selected files appear in Full Screen Preview mode. The files do not appear instantly on the screen, however; CorelDRAW must draw each one layer by layer. Note that complex files may take considerable time to appear fully on the screen.

Adjusting Display Settings for MOSAIC

Purpose

You can adjust the display settings for MOSAIC to customize
your setup. You can choose to display files as icons or in the
more conventional file name list.

Steps

1. Open MOSAIC.

2. From the Special menu, select Preferences. The
   Mosaic: Preferences dialog box appears.

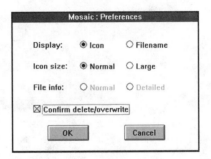

3. Select options from the following settings:

   - **Display.** Enables you to specify whether files are
     displayed by name or by icon. To display a file list,
     click Filename.

   - **Icon size.** If you select Icon from the Display
     options, you can choose to display icons in Normal
     or Large size. Large icon size is helpful if you have
     a large screen display or to distinguish between
     nearly identical files.

   - **File info.** Normal lists only the file name. Detailed
     displays a file list with date, size, and status.

   - **Confirm delete/overwrite.** Enables you to disable
     the warning message that appears whenever
     MOSAIC deletes or overwrites a file. Keep this
     option selected to help prevent files from being
     accidentally lost.

Importing Files

Purpose

CorelDRAW enables you to import and export graphics from a variety of sources, giving you connectivity to other drawing programs, as well as page layout, presentation, spreadsheet and word processing programs.

There are several types of files you can import into CorelDRAW. You might want to insert one drawing file into another, or import a text file into a drawing file, for example.

Steps

1. Select Import from the File menu.

2. In the Import dialog box, select the file format to import. If you selected Use Mosaic under Preferences, the MOSAIC screen will appear. Otherwise, a file selection dialog box will appear.

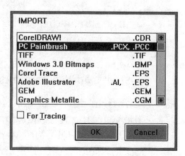

3. Select the desired file, and press Import. You can import the following types of files:

- **CorelDRAW Files.** You can import another CorelDRAW file into the current file. This method is a useful alternative to cutting and pasting, especially with large files. The CorelDRAW file will be imported with all objects grouped together. Ungroup the file to manipulate individual objects.

- **Bit Maps.** To import bit maps, select the bit map format desired. CorelDRAW will import .PCX, .PCC, .TIF and .BMP (Windows bit maps) files.

  The For Tracing option enables you to trace the bit map in CorelDRAW using the Pencil tool. Corel-DRAW will import a higher resolution screen image of the bit map that will not print. See the discussion on tracing later in this chapter. You can trace a bit map with For Tracing turned off, but the tracing will be less accurate because the screen representation is coarser.

  Bit maps can be stretched, scaled, skewed and rotated like any other object. However, any distortion other than a 180-degree rotation or mirror will cause the bit map not to display. A gray square with a white corner will be substituted.

Rotated and skewed bit maps will only print on PostScript printers.

Use Fill to color the white areas of a bit map. If the Fill is set to None, the white areas will be transparent. Use Outline Color to color the black areas of a bit map.

- **CorelTRACE Files**. CorelTRACE produces .EPS files that can be imported into CorelDRAW. The files will consist of a group of objects that can be manipulated like any other objects. The CorelTRACE utility is discussed later in this chapter.

- **Other File Formats**. CorelDRAW can import files from a broad variety of file formats. This allows you to use files created in other vector graphics programs, CADD programs and presentation programs. Due to the differing nature of the various file formats, not all features can be imported. Refer to the *CorelDRAW! Technical Reference* for information regarding specific file formats.

Don't forget the Windows Clipboard! Graphics from other Windows-based programs can usually be imported via the Windows Clipboard, such as Designer files and Excel graphs. There are also a number of third-party utilities that can convert files between various graphic formats. Thus if you have a graphic file that is not directly importable into CorelDRAW, it may be possible to convert it into another format that is supported by CorelDRAW. The *CorelDRAW! Technical Reference* lists several useful software packages. Another is Symsoft's HotShot Graphics.

Exporting Files

Purpose

CorelDRAW can export files in a variety of formats, enabling you to use CorelDRAW files in desktop publishing and word processing programs that do not directly access CorelDRAW files. You can also export CorelDRAW files in bit-map and Macintosh-compatible formats.

Steps

1. Select Export from the File menu. The Export dialog box appears.

```
┌──────────────────────────────────────────────────────────┐
│  EXPORT                                                    │
│  ┌─────────────────────────────────────┐                  │
│  │ CorelDRAW!              .CDR   ▲│                  │
│  │ CorelDRAW! 1.xx         .CDR    │                  │
│  │ Postscript(EPS)         .EPS    │                  │
│  │ Windows Metafile        .WMF    │                  │
│  │ PCX                     .PCX    │                  │
│  │ TIFF                    .TIF   ▼│                  │
│  └─────────────────────────────────────┘                  │
│                                                            │
│  ☐ Selected Object(s) Only    ☒ Include All Artistic Attributes │
│                                                            │
│  ☐ Include Image Header       ☐ All Fonts Resident         │
│                                                            │
│  Resolution:  ○ Coarse(40)  ○ Low(75)  ○ Medium(150)  ○ High(300) │
│                                                            │
│  Fixed Size:  ○ 128X128    ○ 256X256  ○ 512X512            │
│                                                            │
│                              ┌────────┐  ┌────────┐        │
│                              │   OK   │  │ Cancel │        │
│                              └────────┘  └────────┘        │
└──────────────────────────────────────────────────────────┘
```

2. Select the export format from the list box. A file menu appears.

   The following options are available when exporting files. (Some options may not be available for all files):

   - **Selected Objects Only.** Check this box to export only the currently selected objects

   - **Include Image Header.** For .EPS files, this option will include a small bit-map representation of the file that is used by page layout programs such as PageMaker and Ventura to display the imported file. The resolution of the header can be controlled (see Resolution).

- **Include All Artistic Attributes.** Selecting this option exports CorelDRAW's fill and stroke settings, along with other drawing effects. Not all graphic formats support these attributes, however. Turning this off may facilitate the export of certain file formats. See the *Technical Reference* for details.

- **All Fonts Resident.** Checking this causes Corel-DRAW to substitute the resident Adobe printer fonts for the native CorelDRAW fonts when exporting .EPS files. Any typefaces that are not resident in the printer will print in Courier.

- **Resolution.** When creating bit-map files, you must choose one of four resolution settings. The higher the resolution, the sharper the bit-map image will be. However, high-resolution bit-map files can be *very* large, and will take a *long* time to export.

To create a bit map of the minimum size necessary, scale the graphic in CorelDRAW to the final printed size, and then export it at 300 DPI. Make sure you export only the necessary objects; exporting a full page at 300 DPI will create a file of over one megabyte. Make sure your printer has sufficient memory to handle the bit map size.

- **Fixed Size.** Controls the size of the image header for .EPS files. Select a high resoluton if precise positioning is required; otherwise select a low resolution to reduce the file size.

3. Give the export file a name, and press OK. If you don't type in a name, the file will be given the CorelDRAW file name, with the export file extension.

Notes

The bit-map files CorelDRAW creates are monochrome. Colors are converted to dithered patterns of black and white bits.

Use Export in place of Cut and Paste to export all or part of a CorelDRAW file into a new file. Since you are not using the

Windows Clipboard, you will not be subject to it's memory limitations.

Use **E**xport to save CorelDRAW files to the earlier 1.x format. This can be useful when giving files to someone with an earlier version of CorelDRAW. New features introduced in version 2.0, such as bit-map/vector fills, arrowheads and dashed lines will not be exported. Also, typefaces introduced in 2.0 will not show up in 1.x files unless they've been added to the earlier program.

Export is also useful when exporting files to Ventura and PageMaker. It is also useful for exporting files to Macintosh-based service bureaus. Since EPS files are in vector format, they can be scaled without losing image quality, just like CorelDRAW files.

Pantone spot colors are converted to process colors in the EPS format. Some programs, notably Ventura, will not display the image header in the true location of the image; it will be shifted slightly. Exported EPS files cannot be reimported into CorelDRAW. When exporting EPS files for printing by a Macintosh-based service bureau, you may need to turn off the image header for the file to print.

Export provides an easy way of transferring CorelDRAW files to the Macintosh environment for use in applications such as Adobe Illustrator. Select Include All **A**rtistic Attributes (default) when exporting. Not all CorelDRAW features are supported in the .AI format—see the *CorelDRAW! Technical Reference* for details.

Avoid exporting very complex objects if possible. Instead, break the objects apart and reassemble them after exporting. Text should be sent as text, if the font is available in the Macintosh environment. If not, select Send Text as **C**urves. This tends to work better than converting the text to curves in CorelDRAW.

SCODL Format

This export format is used to create high resolution slides. Some color printers use the SCODL format as well. When making slides, make sure that the Page Size is set to **S**lide (11 x 7.33 inches) and the orientation is set to **L**andscape. Keep all objects within the page area. The *CorelDRAW! Technical Reference* describes the requirements for creating SCODL output in detail. Check with your slide-making service as well. Many service bureaus have the capability of making slides directly from CorelDRAW files, giving you access to more PostScript effects than are available in SCODL format.

Windows MetaFile Format

Windows MetaFile is a vector-based format that gives you connectivity to Windows programs supporting the WMF format. However, since this is a non-PostScript format, no PostScript functions are exported. Also, WMF files can be very large if the CorelDRAW file contains lots of text or curves, which may cause problems with Ventura and PageMaker. EPS is a better export choice for complex files.

Exporting radial fountain fills can take a very long time to export to certain file formats. Try replacing the radial fills with blends before exporting.

As with **I**mport, there are certain limitations when exporting CorelDRAW files to other file formats. These are discussed in detail in the *CorelDRAW! Technical Reference*.

Using AutoTrace

Purpose

CorelDRAW provides several ways to trace bit-mapped images. In addition to manually tracing the image, you can use CorelDRAW's AutoTrace feature for simple images. For complex illustrations, and when you want to capture the fine detail of a complex original, use CorelTRACE, which is discussed later in this chapter.

Steps

1. From the <u>F</u>ile menu, select <u>I</u>mport.

2. Check the For <u>T</u>racing box to import a higher-resolution, more detailed screen image.

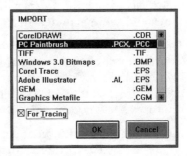

3. Click OK.

4. Select the bit map you want to trace and click OK.

5. Select the Pencil tool. The word AutoTrace appears on the Status Line, and the cursor changes shape.

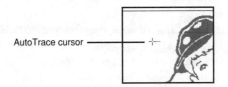

AutoTrace cursor

6. Click on each area of the image that you want to trace. You may need to zoom in to trace small areas. If the area is large or complex, tracing may take some time. If you click on an area where there is nothing to trace, you will get a warning message.

Notes

You can control how the bit map is traced by adjusting the AutoTrace Tracking, Corner Threshold and Straight Line Threshold settings under the Preferences menu.

The AutoTrace function in CorelDRAW is most useful for tracing simple objects, such as logos and typeforms, that will later be edited in CorelDRAW. If you are going to do a lot of node editing, set the AutoTrace Tracking to a high number, to produce as few nodes as possible.

Import as high-resolution a bit map as possible. Scan original art at 300 dpi. If the original image is tiny, try enlarging it on a photocopier before scanning.

 Large bit maps take up a lot of file and memory space, and can be very slow to preview. To speed up work on other parts of the file, AutoTrace only the outline of the bit map to create a place holder, then temporarily "hide" the bit map by exporting it to another file. (Do not cut the bit map to the Clipboard— it will use up too much memory.) After you are finished working on the other objects, you can reimport the bit map.

 After you are finished with a bit map, delete it from the CorelDRAW file to reduce the file size.

Using CorelTRACE

Purpose

The CorelTRACE utility is much more powerful than the AutoTrace function, providing finer control over tracing options. CorelTRACE can trace color and gray-scale images as well as monochrome bit maps.

Because CorelTRACE uses a lot of memory, it is a good idea to shut down other programs before running CorelTRACE.

Steps

1. In Windows, click on the CorelTRACE icon in the CorelDRAW icon in the CorelDRAW Applications Group, which was automatically created when you installed CorelDRAW. The CorelTRACE menu will appear.

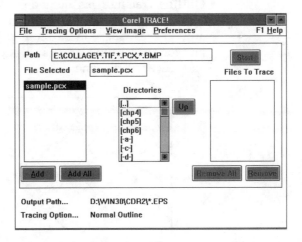

2. Use the Directories box to locate a file or files to trace. Click on the file name to highlight it, and click **A**dd to add it to the list of files to trace. You can select as many files as you want, as long as they are in the same directory.

3. Check the **O**utput Options box under the **F**ile menu. This shows where the traced files will be saved. Select the desired destination, and click OK.

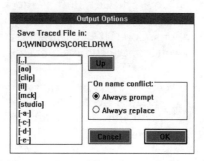

4. Select a **T**racing Option to select one of the default tracing methods, or to create a custom tracing method as discussed in a later section of this chapter.

   There are two default tracing methods in CorelTRACE:

   • **Outline Tracing**. This method works the same as AutoTrace in CorelDRAW, drawing an outline around every shape in the bit map. Outline works best for images with large black and white areas, and few or no fine lines.

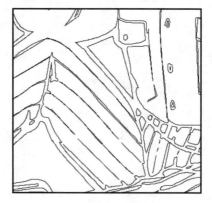

- **Centerline Tracing**. This method traces thin lines as lines, rather than objects. It is best for bit maps with fine lines, such as mechanical drawings and maps.

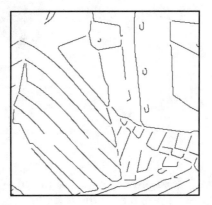

If the bit map you want to trace contains both solids and lines, you may have to try both methods to see which one gives you the best results. Or, you can trace the file both ways, and combine parts in CorelDRAW.

5. If you only want to trace a portion of the bit map, select Trace **P**artial Area from the **P**references menu.

6. Click **S**tart to begin tracing. A tracing window will appear, in which the bit map is drawn.

7. If you have selected Trace **P**artial Area, a cropping box appears. Select the area to trace.

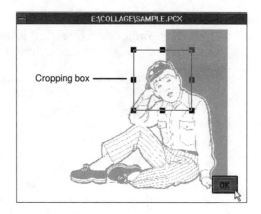

Cropping box

8. Click OK. CorelTRACE then begins tracing. An indicator at the bottom of the window shows the progress of the tracing.

9. To stop tracing, press the Esc key or double-click on the Control Bar icon in the upper left-hand corner of the tracing window.

10. When the tracing is complete, close the tracing window by double-clicking on the Control Bar. You can quit CorelTRACE by selecting Exit from the File menu.

11. The traced images will be saved in the directory you select from the Output Options menu. If you are going to be doing a lot of "test" tracing of the same object, you can change the On Name Conflict setting to Always replace. Otherwise, you will receive a warning prompt before the program overwrites an existing file.

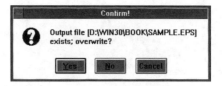

Notes

If you have selected more than one file to trace, they will be traced in sequence.

If you have a one-megabyte or larger RAM drive, copy the bit map files onto it prior to tracing. The files will display much faster. Avoid tracing images on floppy disks; copy them onto the hard drive or a RAM drive first.

Customizing Tracing Options

Purpose

You can create your own custom tracing setup in CorelTRACE to control various tracing options.

Steps

1. Double-click on one of the blank lines in the Tracing Options menu. The Tracing Options dialog box appears.

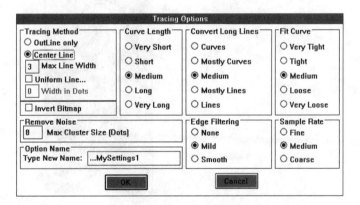

2. Select settings from the following options:

   • **Tracing Method.** You can choose either OutLine only or Center Line. For Center Line, you can control the line thickness, from 2 to 99 pixels. Set this to the average thickness in points of the lines in the bit map. If the lines are much wider than 6 points, use OutLine only tracing instead.

- **Uniform Line.** When checked, this option sets all the lines to the same thickness, from 1 to 99 dots.

Non-uniform line   Uniform line

- **Invert Bitmap.** This option will reverse the black and white areas of the bit map prior to tracing.

- **Remove Noise.** This setting causes CorelTRACE to ignore areas smaller than the specified size in pixels. This is useful for getting rid of "dirt" in the bit map, or reducing the level of detail. You can set the cluster size from 2 to 999 pixels.

- **Curve Length.** This controls the length of the curves generated by CorelTRACE. The shorter the curve length, the more nodes will be created. To trace the bit map more precisely, however, you will also have to adjust Fit Curve and Sample Rate.

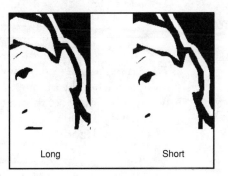

Long   Short

- **Convert Long Lines.** This controls how CorelTRACE converts long lines. For bit maps consisting of straight lines, such as architectural plans, this would be set to Lines. For rounded objects, this would be set to Curves.

| Lines | Curves |

- **Edge Filtering.** This determines how sharp edges are handled. None traces them as closely as possible. Smooth rounds them off.

| None | Smooth |

- **Fit Curve.** This determines how closely the traced image matches the bit map. If you want to smooth out a ragged bit map, set this to Loose or Very Loose. Alternately, if you want to pick up every bump, set this to Very Tight.

- **Sample Rate.** This works in a similar fashion as Fit Curve. A Fine setting will follow the bit map precisely, and a Coarse setting will produce a less accurate tracing.

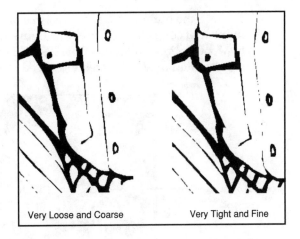

Very Loose and Coarse   Very Tight and Fine

- **Option Name.** Give your custom setting a name and click OK.

Do not edit either of the default settings, or they will be overwritten.

Color Reduction Settings

The **C**olor Reduction settings found in the **P**references menu controls the number of colors or gray levels that CorelTRACE uses to fill the traced image.

Color Reduction Scheme

Reduce colors to ...   8   Colors

Reduce grays to ...   64 Gray levels

☐ Convert to Mono

Cancel   OK

To trace the outline of a shape, it is usually better to set the number of colors or grays to a low figure, or use the Convert to Mono option. The colors CorelTRACE uses are from fixed palettes, and may not match the traced object exactly.

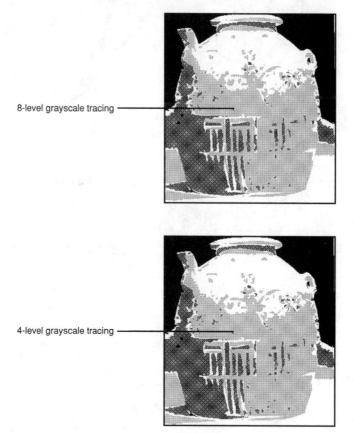

8-level grayscale tracing

4-level grayscale tracing

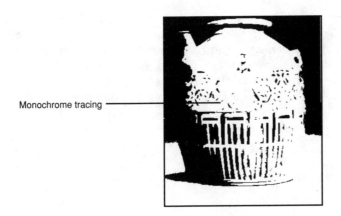

Monochrome tracing

Using CorelTRACE Images

CorelTRACE generates EPS files that must be imported into CorelDRAW to be edited. Because they are EPS files, they can sometimes be imported directly into programs that support EPS files, such as Ventura and PageMaker. However, CorelTRACE files do not have an image header, so you cannot see them on-screen in these programs.

To edit a CorelTRACE file, import it into CorelDRAW. All the objects will be grouped together, so you will have to ungroup them to work on individual elements. The objects will be saved as normal CorelDRAW objects when the CorelDRAW file is saved.

Fine Tuning Tracings

Trial and error is the best way to find the optimum tracing settings for any given image. Decide whether you want to follow a bit map exactly or smooth out its irregularities. Use Trace Partial Area to test various settings before you trace the entire bit map. The CorelTRACE manual shows a number of samples that will help you choose the optimum tracing settings. When you find a suitable method, save it as a custom setting.

Very large or very complex bit maps can consume a lot of memory and may sometimes exceed the space available in your TEMP directory. You will get an error message if this happens. CorelTRACE needs a TEMP directory space about 10 times the size of the bit map to convert an image.

Tracing Manually

Purpose

Even though CorelDRAW has two fine tracing tools, it is sometimes quicker or more convenient to trace an object manually. For instance, if you want to create final art from a rough sketch of a logo, a CorelTRACE or AutoTrace of the bit map is not of much use, as a large number of nodes are generated that you will end up deleting to create the final art.

Steps

1. Import the bit map into a CorelDRAW file with For Tracing selected to get a high-resolution image, but leave it unhighlighted so you do not activate the AutoTrace function.

2. With the pen tool, draw straight lines where you will need to create nodes. Do not draw curves now—you will make them from the straight lines later.

3. If there are any ellipses or rectangles in the design, draw these with the appropriate tools.

4. When you have finished drawing lines, combine them all, and use Convert to Curves where needed.

5. Edit the curves to match the bit map. When you are finished, you can break the curves apart as necessary.

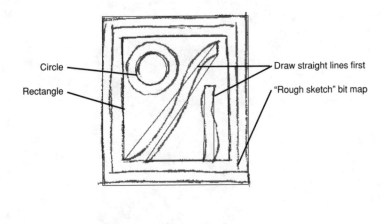

Circle

Rectangle

Draw straight lines first

"Rough sketch" bit map

Index

O

objects
  aligning, 9-11, 116-118
  closing, 28
  combining, 108
  copying, 89, 93-97
  deselecting, 16-17
  duplicate, 20
  filling, 28
  flipping, 92
  free-form, 39
  grouping, 106
  moving, 87-89
  multiple
    moving, 88
    selecting, 16-17
  nudging, 90
  placing, 113, 116
  primary, 39
  redrawing, 88
  rotating, 96-99
  selecting, 14-15
  skewing, 96, 100-101
  stretching, 91-93, 96, 169
Offsets command, 131-133
one-point perspective, 173
Open command, 7, 133, 196
opening files, 7
options
  Curve Length, 219
  Edge Filtering, 220
  Fit Curve, 220
  Line Cap, 123
  Reinstall Fonts, 79
  Sample Rate, 220
  Set Kern, 79
  Slide, 8
  Smooth, 37
  Source Directory, 77
  Spot color, 137
  Symmet, 37
  Tabloid, 8
  to Curve, 37
  to Line, 34
  Tracing Method, 217
  see also, commands

Options button, 136
Options menu, 78-79
Others button, 143
Outline Color dialog box, 140
Outline menu, 121, 126
outline pen, 120-121
Outline Pen dialog box, 121, 126
Outline tool, 6, 120-121, 126, 139
outline tracing, 214
outlines, 119
  copying, 149
  creating, 71
  default, 147
  editing, 121-126
  shading, 121
  width, 120-121
Output Options box, 214
Output Options menu, 216
Overprint command, 150

P

page orientation, 7
Page Setup command, 8
Page Setup dialog box, 8
palettes, 165
Pantone Matching System (PMS), 140
Paragraph text (text type), 47
Paragraph text mode, 56
paragraphs
  spacing, 57
  text, 60
parallel extrusion, 153-154
Paste button, 49
Paste command, 21, 208
pasting text, 49
PAT files, 133
paths, 63
Pen tools, 224
Pencil tool, 6, 25-29, 211
perspective, 173-178
Perspective check box, 155
Perspective command, 55, 60, 112, 153

Z

New Riders Puts You on the Cutting Edge of Computer Information!

AUTOCAD

AutoCAD: The Professional Reference $39.95
AutoCAD: Drafting and 3D Design $29.95
AutoCAD: Drafting and 3D Design Disk $14.95
AutoCAD: Drafting and 3D Design
  Instructor's Guide $175.00
AutoCAD 3D Design and Presentation $29.95
AutoCAD for Beginners $19.95
AutoCAD Instructor's Guide $175.00
AutoCAD Reference Guide, 2nd Edition $14.95
AutoCAD Student Workbook $39.95
AutoCAD Windows for Beginners $19.95
Inside AutoCAD, Special Edition $34.95
Inside AutoCAD Release 11, Metric Edition $34.95
Inside AutoCAD Windows $34.95
Maximizing AutoCAD, Volume I:
  Customizing AutoCAD with Macros & Menus ... $34.95
Maximizing AutoCAD, Volume II:
  Inside AutoLISP $34.95
Managing and Networking AutoCAD $29.95

ENTERPRISE COMPUTING

Enterprise Series: Applications $39.95
Enterprise Series: Connectivity $39.95
Enterprise Series: Operating Systems $39.95

GRAPHICS

CorelDRAW! On Command $19.95
Inside Autodesk Animator $29.95
Inside AutoSketch, 2nd Edition $24.95
Inside CorelDRAW!, 2nd Edition $29.95
Inside CorelDRAW!, 3rd Edition $34.95
Inside Generic CADD $29.95

OPERATING SYSTEMS/NETWORKING/MISC.

Inside CompuServe $29.95
Inside LAN Manager $34.95
Inside Novell NetWare $29.95
Inside OS/2, Release 2.0 .... $34.95
Inside SCO UNIX $29.95
Inside Solaris SunOS $29.95
Inside Windows 3.1 .... $29.95
Managing Novell NetWare $39.95
Maximizing MS-DOS 5 .... $34.95
Maximizing Windows 3 .... $39.95
Maximizing Windows 3.1 .... $39.95
Novell NetWare On Command $19.95
UNIX On Command $19.95
Windows 3.1 Networking $22.95
Windows 3 On Command $19.95
Windows 3.1 On Command $19.95

NRP
NEW RIDERS
PUBLISHING

For More Information, Call Toll-Free
1-800-428-5331

All prices and titles are subject to change without notice. Non-U.S. prices may be higher. Printed in the U.S.A.

New Riders Gives You
Maximum AutoCAD Performance!